30776

The
LC20

Davi   D0609569

THE HIGHER EDUCATION

OF WOMEN

(1866)

THE HIGHER EDUCATION

OF WOMEN

(1866)

By EMILY DAVIES

EDITED WITH AN INTRODUCTION

BY JANET HOWARTH

THE HAMBLEDON PRESS
LONDON   AND   RONCEVERTE

Published by the Hambledon Press, 1988

102 Gloucester Avenue,
London NW1 8HX (U.K.)

309 Greenbrier Avenue,
Ronceverte WV 24970 (U.S.A.)

ISBN 1 85285 008 6 (cased)
     1 85285 009 4 (paper)

British Library Cataloguing in Publication Data

Davies, Emily
   The higher education of women (1866).
   1. Higher education of women—Great
   Britain
   I. Title
376'.65'0941   LC2046

Printed and bound by WBC, Bristol and Maesteg

30776

CONTENTS

ACKNOWLEDGEMENTS

I would like to thank the Mistress and Fellows of Girton College for permission to quote from the Emily Davies papers and in particular Girton's archivist, Mrs. Kate Perry, for her invaluable assistance and advice. Among the many colleagues who have helped me to find a perspective on Miss Davies and her book my thanks are especially due to those who answered specific queries, Kate Duncan Jones, Daniel Karlin, Kate Lilley, Colin Matthew and Anne Summers, and to Mark Curthoys whose comments on an early draft of the introduction prompted some major revisions. Any remaining errors are my responsibility alone.

INTRODUCTION

BY JANET HOWARTH

'THERE is no subject of vital human concern about which public opinion has changed so much in the last seventy years as it has about the education of women. The alteration has come about gradually, but not spontaneously; it is a result of the ardent efforts of a few small groups of devoted men and women'. Sarah Emily

Davies (1830-1921), whose biography prompted these comments,[1] was among those promoters of change. She is remembered chiefly as founder of Girton, the first of the Cambridge and Oxford women's colleges, which started in a house at Hitchin in 1869 and moved to Cambridge in 1873. Yet in the decade before Girton opened she had already made a major contribution as committee woman and publicist to the cause of women's education and it was she who, together with Elizabeth Garrett, delivered to John Stuart Mill, M.P. for Westminster, the first women's suffrage petition, presented to parliament in 1866. *The Higher Education of Women*, published in the same year, was the work of a central figure in the mid-Victorian women's movement and one who was convinced that time was on its side.

The debate on the position of women to which this book belongs began in the late eighteenth century when Mary Wollstonecraft's *Vindication of the Rights of Women* (1792), inspired by the egalitarianism of the French revolution, brought a hostile reponse from Evangelical writers concerned to defend the patriarchal traditions of canon law and to prescribe for women a distinct and subordinate role within the family.[2] Where Wollstonecraft claimed equal rights for women as autonomous moral beings, including the right to work, Hannah More asserted that 'the profession of ladies ... is that of daughters, wives, mothers and mistresses of families'.[3] Egalitarian feminism continued to find support in groups on the fringes of conventional society – Unitarians, philosophic radicals, the Owenite socialists of the 1830s. But evangelical influences increasingly affected the treatment of women's roles in early nineteenth-century tracts and manuals, the periodical press, novels and poetry. Secular trends reinforced their message. To women belonged a special place in the formation of life-styles in the rapidly growing business and professional classes, as guardians of domestic manners, morals and comforts. Industrialisation and urbanisation, the separation of home from work-place and the rise of a consumer society created new boundaries between male and female spheres. Mid-Victorian positivists, influenced by Darwin's theory of evolution, stressed the eugenic significance of women's reproductive functions as the key to the fitness of the race and suggested a causal link between the high level of civilisation attained by English society and the clear differentiation of gender roles.[4] The education of boys and girls, particularly in the middle and upper classes, differed accordingly. The regime of the Victorian public school, which stressed 'manly' qualities, mental discipline and systematic learning, increasingly monitored by examinations, contrasted with the more haphazard way in which daughters were prepared for feminine roles, by parents or governesses at home or in small private schools which placed 'accomplishments' before intellectual attainment.[5]

Yet the notion of woman as exclusively a creature of home and family was never unproblematic, even within the middle classes: it corresponded neither with social realities nor with the religious ideals of nineteenth-century Anglicanism. Many women did, in practice, earn their own livings: Hannah More herself was a self-supporting writer. Middle-class incomes were often too low and too precarious to guarantee support for widows and unmarried daughters. The growing surplus of women in the population ensured that many would never have the opportunity of marriage. The convention inherited from the eighteenth century, that no 'lady' could work for payment without losing her genteel status, and the lack of appropriate education or training to prepare girls from middle-class homes who needed to support themselves, created actual hardship and touched humanitarian consciences. It was an Anglican initiative . to improve the education of governesses, led by the Broad Church theologian and Christian Socialist F. D. Maurice, that founded Queen's College, Harley Street in 1848. But the demand for women's education and employment came not only from those in material need. The evangelicals' emphasis on the work ethic and the duty of self-examination encouraged a critical perspective on the actualities of women's lives. Maria Grey and Emily Shirreff, whose *Thoughts on Self-Culture addressed to Women* were published in 1850, did not question the prior claim on women of family duties, yet they had experienced 'as young girls on the threshold of life' a 'painful sense of inconsistency between life as it appeared in reality, and the religious theory of life'. For unmarried daughters in the servant-keeping households of their generation there were few opportunities for Christian service within the family but they lacked the education to conceive of 'some comprehensive principle by which to regulate thought and action . . . some real aim for exertion'.[6] The dilemma of the conscientious home daughter was summed up by Emily Davies in a memorable phrase: 'the case of the modern girl is peculiarly hard in this, that she has fallen upon an age in which idleness is accounted disgraceful'.[7] Nor was it necessary to believe in the equality of the sexes to question conventions that allocated to women important tasks, including the training of young children, charitable work and a presiding role in the drawing rooms of cultivated families, yet treated their education as unimportant and their mental powers as inferior. 'The discussions about equality always seem to me extremely barren and tiresome', wrote Miss Davies. 'I don't the least in the world mind being called inferior on behalf of women in general, except insofar as that continually telling people that they cannot do things is apt to make them incapable, and in the interest of the human race it is not desirable for women to believe e.g. that they *cannot* be reasonable'.[8]

Emily Davies was influenced both by religious currents within the Anglican Church and by the feminist tradition that derived from Mary Wollstonecraft. The daughter of a clergyman, she recalled a 'feeling of resentment at the subjection of women' that grew out of her own experience long before she encountered feminist ideas.[9] John Davies (1795-1861), a Welsh farmer's son and Cambridge graduate, exemplified the evangelical call to active virtue. Until his health was affected by overwork he combined the care of a Chichester parish and a boarding school for boys with literary work that included tracts against Sabbath breaking and Popish doctrine and a philosophical treatise of some distinction, *An Estimate of the Human Mind* (1828). Emily's childhood memories were of a shared family religious and intellectual life. She played with her sister and three brothers at holding missionary meetings and being a candidate for parliament, and compiled newspapers of strongly Conservative tone, filled with denunciations of Popery and Puseyism. She also shared enough of her brothers' early education to whet her appetite for more, writing weekly essays that were looked over by her father and learning Latin for pleasure 'simply because the boys were doing it'.[10] But when

John Davies became rector of Gateshead in Durham in 1839 he excluded girls from the grammar school that was held in a room over the vestry, believing that their presence 'lowered the status of the school'.[11] Emily attended a girls' day school for only a few months: beyond that, she had lessons with her mother or elder sister and with visiting masters who taught French, Italian and music. Meanwhile her elder brothers, destined for the Church, were sent to Repton and Cambridge while the youngest went to Arnold's Rugby and into a solicitor's office. Her own life, once the boys had left home, narrowed to a routine of home duties and parish work – visiting the poor and a little teaching – for which she had neither taste nor training, combined with sporadic reading and attempts to teach herself languages. In these Gateshead years she formed friendships with like-minded young women, Jane Crow and Elizabeth Garrett, who came to share her aspirations for a more fulfilling life. At the same time her brother Llewelyn was drawn, as a curate in East London's East End in the 1850s, into the Christian Socialist circle of F. D. Maurice and Charles Kingsley, whose social concern extended to the position of women.[12] But it was not until Emily was twenty-eight that she happened to meet, on a visit to an invalid brother in Algiers, two decidedly unconventional women, Annie Leigh Smith and her sister Barbara Bodichon, illegitimate daughters of the

Unitarian Radical M.P. Benjamin Leigh
Smith and active feminists, who gave her
for the first time encouragement to articu-
late her own discontents and work for
change.

Barbara Bodichon (1827-1891), a gifted
painter with a comfortable private income,
and her friend Bessie Rayner Parkes
(Mme Belloc, 1829-1925), also daughter of
a Radical Unitarian, Joseph Parkes of
Birmingham, were founding members of
England's first organised women's movement, a movement that briefly drew
together women from a variety of religious, political and social backgrounds.[13]
Its centre, at 19 Langham Place in the
suburbs of North London, housed the
offices of the *English Woman's Journal*

(launched in March 1858) and the Society For Promoting the Employment of Women as well as a ladies' club with a reading room and dining room. The cohesion of this movement was fragile. The *Journal* ran into financial problems and ceased publication in 1864; the women's suffrage movement, formed during the debates over parliamentary reform in 1865-7, came under the leadership of Radicals, such as J. S. Mill's step-daughter Helen Taylor, and alienated women who did not share their politics; others were alienated by the opening in the later 1860s of questions of sexual politics such as birth control and the Contagious Diseases Acts which regulated prostitution. But the publications, committees and informal networks connected with the Langham Place centre had, in their day, a powerful influence in challenging received thinking about the position of women and promoting reform.

Mid-Victorian public opinion was not slow to take interest in 'women's questions', as Mme Bodichon had found in her efforts to secure reform of the law that denied married women the right to own property. A petition she drafted in 1856 attracted over 24,000 signatures and the backing of Lord Brougham and the Law Amendment Society. The National Association for the Promotion of Social Science, founded in 1857, drew at its annual congresses on the expertise of women as well as men and it formed close ties with the Langham Place set. Among the members of the Social Science Association were men who had already advanced the cause of women, including Brougham, Maurice and J. S. Mill, a long-standing advocate of women's suffrage. Others were to become weighty allies, notably Lord Lyttelton, Henry Roby and Joshua Fitch, key figures in the Schools' Inquiry Commission which investigated middle-class education in 1864-8. While the *English Woman's Journal* created new links between feminists and women active in public life – 'threaded the separate parts of the movements, brought the thinkers and the workers together'[14] – the Social Science Association gave them access to leaders of contemporary opinion who were receptive to much that they had to say.

Emily Davies first visited Langham
Place in 1859 and, on returning to Gateshead, found no difficulty in arousing
interest in the women's movement in her
own provincial circles too. When she
started a North-Eastern branch of the
S.P.E.W. influential people gave support
and a local paper published her comments
on women's employment in the region.[15]
Elizabeth Garrett was persuaded to follow
the example of the pioneering American,
Elizabeth Blackwell, and train as a doctor,
and Jane Crow became secretary of the
S.P.E.W. and went to live at Langham
Place. When John Davies died in 1861,
leaving Emily a modest independent income, she moved with her mother to
London and was free to play a more

prominent part in the movement. She acted in 1862-3 as editor of the *English Woman's Journal*, then of the *Victoria Magazine*, a product of Emily Faithfull's Victoria Press, a printing firm staffed by women. She published articles on women's education and employment and papers by her were read at Social Science Congresses.[16] But her chief contribution to the cause was to be as a 'worker' rather than a 'thinker'.

Miss Davies' talent for lobbying and committee work was revealed in a series of campaigns on educational issues, prompted initially by Elizabeth Garrett's difficulties in gaining access to medical training.[17] She began by organising a memorial to persuade London University,

on the renewal of its charter in 1862, to
admit women to degrees. The near success
of this move (rejected in the Senate only
by the Chancellor's casting vote) encouraged the formation of a committee, with
Miss Davies as secretary, to work for the
admission of women to university examinations elsewhere, including the local
examinations for schoolboys started by
Oxford and Cambridge in the 1850s (the
precursors of G.C.E. 'O' and 'A' levels).
This project brought her into contact with
women associated with the few girls'
schools that offered a sound academic
education, notably Dorothea Beale of
Cheltenham Ladies' College, Frances
Mary Buss of North London Collegiate
School and Miss Bostock of Bedford

College (a Unitarian foundation dating from 1849, later to become part of London University but at this stage a secondary school). London's degrees remained closed to women until 1878 but important advances for girls' secondary education were achieved by Miss Davies and her committee. Cambridge admitted girls to its local examinations, first on an experimental basis in 1863 but permanently from 1865: Edinburgh and Durham and eventually, in 1870, Oxford followed suit. A still more productive step was taken when Emily Davies' persistent lobbying persuaded the Schools' Inquiry Commissioners to include girls' schools in their investigations. The nine ladies called as witnesses, herself among them, were the first to give evidence in person to a Royal Commission,[18] while the subcommissioners' reports prepared for this enquiry were the first survey undertaken of the schooling of middle-class girls: 'the Doomsday Book of women's education', as Maria Grey described it, 'recording, however, not its possessions but its deficiencies'.[19] The outcome was a recommendation, endorsed by parliament in the 1869 Endowed Schools Act, that in the reform of ancient educational endowments money should be made available for the foundation of grammar schools for girls as well as boys, and an upsurge of public interest in girls' education that produced many voluntary initiatives, including the formation of the Girls' Public Day School Company (1872).

In these years Emily Davies also acted as
honorary secretary to two other bodies
with a significant place in the women's
movement: the Kensington Society, formed in 1865 to discuss social and political
questions, whose members placed women's
suffrage on the agenda of parliamentary
reform; and the London Schoolmistresses'
Association, which became in 1866 the first
professional body for women schoolteachers. In 1870 she was among the first
four women to be elected as members of
School Boards.

Yet Miss Davies' chief personal concern,
rooted in the frustrations of her early
adult life, was to gain access to university
education for women over eighteen,
particularly those whose genteel back-

grounds fitted them for 'the education of a
lady' rather than the narrowly vocational
training provided in teacher training colleges and nursing schools.[20] *The Higher
Education of Women* was written at a
time when it was still unclear just how
this objective could be realised but when
the climate of opinion, prepared by two
decades of debate on educational reform,
seemed receptive to the principles involved. The value of a good general or
'liberal' education in training character as
well as intellect was emphasised by university and public school reformers, and
the press had been friendly to Emily
Shirreff's suggestion, in a book published
in 1858, that it would benefit wives and
mothers too.[21] Equally attuned to the

orthodoxies of the day was the argument
for free trade in knowledge between the
sexes made in Frances Power Cobbe's plea
for 'University Degrees for Women' at the
1862 Social Science Congress.[22] Emily
Davies herself had already made capital,
in the aftermath of the Newcastle
Commission on elementary education,
from the paradox that government showed
more concern for the education of working
class girls than for the needs of women of
her own social class.[23] It is possible that
her book was an expanded version of a
paper intended for, but not read at, the
1865 Social Science Congress. At all
events, she found in Alexander Strahan a
publisher willing to take on the book at his
own risk: as she recalled, 'I paid nothing,

and received nothing, except a good many copies for giving away'. [24] Strahan's imprint associated the book with a publisher who produced a number of Broad Church and liberal periodicals, including *Good Words*, the *Sunday Magazine* and the *Contemporary Review*, and who was credited by one of his editors with 'a remarkable instinct (for) what would take the public taste'.[25]

The book draws on both the lessons of her Anglican upbringing and the common stock of ideas current in Langham Place and the Kensington Society in the 1860s, many of which in their turn derived from the writings of earlier feminists.[26] It begins by dwelling on the contradictory ideals of woman expressed in contemporary culture. The church set up tensions between the universalism of Christian ethics and the dualism of idealised masculine and feminine virtue, and between women's duty to God and their duty to family. Poets of the generation of Tennyson and Coventry Patmore, novelists and men of letters seemed increasingly to differ about what they wanted of women. Meanwhile few men were aware of the emptiness of the lives many women were compelled to lead. 'Nobody *can* more correctly lay down the symptoms of the moral and mental disease which now disfigures female existence', was the comment of a fellow-member of the Kensington Society.[27] Miss Davies' proposals for change go on to develop arguments used in previous publications on women's work and education by the Langham Place group.[28] Her concern, unlike that of the S.P.E.W., was restricted to the middle classes but there is a characteristic emphasis on the need to open employment to women and see their education as more than a preparation for family roles. Her most tentative chapter was that which reviewed 'specific suggestions' for opening higher education to women, its caution dictated perhaps by the fact that the Schools' Inquiry Commission's deliberations and negotiations with London and other universities were still in progress. The concluding chapter, however, boldly asserts the need to challenge conventional gender roles and distinguish between the natural differences between men and women and artificial ideals of masculinity and feminity. Her attack on the tyranny of custom and the anomalous treatment of women in a society professing civilised values echoes arguments used in J. S. Mills' *Essay on the Subjection of Women*, written in 1861 but not published until 1869. This chapter in particular Helen Taylor praised as 'admirably expressed and as clearly thought', adding, 'It will be well that the matter of this should sink into many half-prepared minds, and when it has had time to do its work you can carry out the same ideas still further'.[29]

'No change could be greater or more desirable than that which would be brought about by the measures she advo-

cates', was the *Westminster Review*'s ver-
dict on the book. 'There is so much
temperance, good sense and originality in
her treatment of the question that it
would be a most regrettable thing if she
failed to ensure a wide circle of readers'.[30]
The book was widely reviewed in the daily
and periodical press and won praise even
in journals not noted for feminist sympathies. 'The first impression produced by
the perusal of this remarkable little book
is one of surprise at the studiously
dispassionate language and the short,
clear, logical sentences which characterise
it; the second, that we could feel no
objection to be prescribed for, nursed,
ruled, to be voted for, or even against,
by a woman who writes in this style',

declared the *Pall Mall Gazette*.[31] *The Spectator*, too, endorsed Miss Davies' case for improving the education of middle-class women. 'On the whole we heartily agree with her that no artificial restrictions should be put on girls' professional leanings, and that parents ought, whenever they can, to train girls for some other calling besides that of the "mother of a family". Half the misery of life to women is caused by their having no specific end to follow ... and the other half caused by making marriage an end in itself to be pursued professionally for its consequences if it cannot be gained by the natural path of falling in love'.[32] But the reviewer went on to express the uneasiness created by Miss Davies' claim for

equal opportunities for women in education and professional life. 'We do not
think she is right in supposing that the
kind of general education which is best for
men would be the best for women also.
Though *intellect* has no gender, *capacity*
probably has, and the stronger capacities
of average women are usually not the
stronger capacities of average men'. Few
women, he thought, would in practice take
to professional work. 'We should be heartily opposed to this movement were it really
likely, as many people suppose it is, to
educate women into pushing, go-ahead,
main-chance-studying females.' Particularly controversial was the suggestion that
professional women might continue to
work after marriage. 'The ultimate result

of so great a change would be a complete revolution of the marital relations', commented the *Westminster Review*. Marriage between fellow-professionals must become a true partnership grounded in personal sympathy, leaving no place for the double standard that countenanced a husband's extra-marital liaisons. 'This is as much a man's question as a woman's and is only shirked because its solution calls for as much reformation in masculine conduct as in female education.'

Outright opposition to women's higher education persisted for many years, especially among the more hidebound members of the church and the medical profession,[33] yet opinion did shift perceptibly in its favour in the later 1860s. 'A kind of general feeling that it was not in accordance with the fitness of things'[34] gave ground to a sense, even in conservative circles, that it was (unlike female suffrage) among those aspects of women's rights that did not 'strike reasonable people as absurd'.[35] Committees sprang up in London and the provinces to organise schemes of lectures for ladies in conjunction with the university extension movement, and special university-level examinations for women over eighteen were started by London (1868), Cambridge (1869) and Oxford (1877).[36] At this point, however, Miss Davies took her stand on the principle that was to associate her name with 'uncompromising' feminism, that the higher education of women must

above all things be the same as that of
men   and   tested   by   the   same
examinations.[37] In 1866 her hopes were
still pinned on transforming Queen's College into a university college for women
over eighteen who would take London
degrees; when that scheme failed, she
assembled a committee to found a new
college for women, associating it instead
with Cambridge where prospects seemed
best for securing admission to undergraduate examinations. The first three Girton
pioneers took Tripos by private arrangement with the examiners in 1873.

In one sense, this strategy proved an
unqualified success. As Miss Davies'
contacts with schoolmistresses had shown,
there was a demand for women's colleges

bearing the same relationship to good girls' schools as the universities did to boys' public schools: within less than three decades Girton was joined by a second Cambridge women's college, Newnham (1871); four more at Oxford, Lady Margaret Hall and Somerville (1879), St Hugh's (1886) and St Hilda's (1893); and two new foundations in London, Westfield (1882) and Royal Holloway (1887).[38] Nor did special examinations for women last long: they were dropped by London in 1878, by Cambridge in 1881 and at Oxford by stages after 1884 as women were admitted to undergraduate examinations on the same terms as men.[39] But Miss Davies' single-minded – even 'one-ideaed'[40] – insistence on equality of the sexes brought her into conflict with early students at Girton as well as influential supporters of women's education at Cambridge and elsewhere. Girtonians were not merely permitted but required to follow the same curriculum and timetable as Cambridge men, although few had had the schooling in classics or mathematics to keep up with Cambridge courses without severe strain. Miss Davies treated her students, Louisa Lumsden complained, as 'a mere cog in the wheel of her great enterprise.... It was plain that we counted for little or nothing except as we furthered her plans'.[41] Equally critical were Cambridge reformers, including Henry Sidgwick of Newnham, who saw no value in subjecting women to a university curriculum that still included compulsory Greek and badly needed modernising. Miss Davies' premature bid in 1887-8 to force Cambridge to admit women to the B.A. degree, before the curriculum had been reformed, divided Girton and Newnham supporters and may have reinforced local prejudices against women. By her death in 1921, Cambridge was the only British university to deny them full membership.[42]

Emily Davies' doctrinaire qualities sprang less from coherent feminist theory than from a conservatism that is evident in her book, with its insistence that the education of a gentleman, as conceived by the public schools and universities, was also the best education for a lady. Herself no teacher or scholar but a 'middle-

woman'[43] in the movement for women's
education, she stood outside the broader
debate on educational reform in which
contemporaries questioned the orthodoxies
of the liberal education, above all its
heavily classical bias. Nor was she among
those creative women who experienced in
their own lives tensions between family
commitments and work that were aggra-
vated by pressure to conform to the norms
of a man's world.[44] She identified chiefly
with the cause of the professional woman,
the schoolmistress or aspiring doctor, who
needed to demonstrate that her qualifications were not inferior to those of men.
But there was irony in the fact that Miss
Davies' egalitarian approach to educational
issues came to be seen as feminist intran-

sigence, since she always maintained a
distaste for 'hard-hitting' or unconventional feminism and a certain detachment
from allies who embraced it. In her own
words, 'I don't think I belong to any
"body", except the Church and two or
three Committees'.[45]

The interest of Emily Davies' book lies
chiefly in the light it throws on the varied
influences that went to shape the mid-
Victorian women's movement, Anglican as
well as radical, conventional and unconventional, although it is also a classic
statement of the case for opening educational and professional opportunities to
women. A variety of initiatives, not all of
them feminist, was to translate her objec-
tives into practice in the years that

followed. But in that process Miss Davies played a catalytic and often far-sighted role, with a force of character and organising ability that, on balance, undoubtedly accelerated the progress of the movement for women's education. 'If Emily Davies had not existed, she would have needed to be invented.'[46]

1. *The Times*, 18 February 1927, review of Barbara Stephen, *Emily Davies and Girton College* (1927). More recent assessments of Emily Davies are given in M.C. Bradbrook, *'That Infidel Place'. A Short History of Girton College 1869-1969* (1969) and M. Forster, *Significant Sisters, The Grassroots of Active Feminism, 1839-1939* (1984).

2. See C. Hall, 'The Early Formation of Victorian Domestic Ideology', in S. Burman (ed.), *Fit Work for*

women (1979); L. Davidoff and C. Hall, *Family Fortunes. Men and Women of the English Middle Class 1780-1850* (1987), pp.71-192.

3. H. More, *Strictures on the Modern System of Female Education* (5th edn., 1800), p.72.

4. L. Duffin, 'Prisoners of Progress: Women and Evolution', in S. Delamont and L. Duffin (eds.), *The Nineteenth Century Woman. Her Cultural and Physical World* (1978).

5. See D. Gorham, *The Victorian Girl and the Feminine Ideal* (1982); F. Hunt (ed.), *Lessons for Life. The Schooling of Girls and Women 1850-1950* (Oxford, 1987).

6. P. vi. This book, which went into a second edition, hints in more temperate language at the frustrations that led Florence Nightingale (1820-1910) to denouce the tyranny of the family; see 'Cassandra', first published in Ray Strachey, *The Cause. A Short History of the Women's Movement in Great Britain* (1928) but privately printed in 1859.

The Shirreff sisters, Emily (1814-97) and Maria (1816-1906), were founders of the Women's Education Union (1871) which launched the Girls' Public Day School Trust and the Teachers' Training and Registration Society; Emily was briefly Mistress of Girton in 1870. Both sisters were too preoccupied with family duties to become involved in the women's movement in the 1860s. See E.W. Ellsworth, *Liberators of the Female Mind. The Shirreff Sisters, Educational Reform and the Women's Movement* (1979).

7. Below, p.44.

8. Letter to R.H. Hutton, n.d.1866, in E. Davies' manuscript 'Family Chronicle', ff.467-8, Girton College archive.

9. Stephen, *Emily Davies*, p.29.

10. *Ibid*, p.25.

11. 'Family Chronicle', f.64.

12. John Llewellyn Davies (1826-1916) became a strong supporter of the women's movement and principal of Queen's College, Harley Street (1872-3 and 1878-86). His daughter Margaret was for many years secretary to the Women's Co-operative Guild.

13. See Strachey, *The Cause*; Lee Holcombe, *Wives and Property* (Oxford, 1983); Jane Rendall, '"A Moral Engine?" Feminism, Liberalism and the *English Women's Journal*', in J. Rendall (ed.), *Equal or Different? Women's Politics, 1800-1914* (Oxford, 1987).

14. Bessie Parkes' phrase, quoted in Rendall, '"A Moral Engine?"', p.112. On the connections between the Social Science Association and the women's movement, see Sheila Fletcher, *Feminists and Bureaucrats, A Study of the Development of Girls' Education in the Nineteenth Century* (Cambridge, 1980).

15. 'Letters addressed to a Daily Paper at Newcastle upon Tyne', 1860, reprinted in E. Davies, *Thoughts on Some Questions Relating to Women, 1860-1908* (1910).

16. 'Medicine as a Profession for Women', 1862; 'Secondary Instruction as Relating to Girls', 1864; 'The Application of Funds to the Education of Girls', 1865.

17. Described in J. Manton, *Elizabeth Garrett Anderson* (1965).

18. Florence Nightingale gave written evidence to the Royal Commission of 1857 on the health of the army. Women had, of course, been interviewed by the subcommissioners who collected evidence for Royal Commissions on social questions in the 1830s and after, and had also given evidence in person to parliamentary committees of inquiry.

19. Ellsworth, *Liberators of the Female Mind*, p.125. See D. Beale (ed.), *Reports issued by the Schools' Inquiry Commission on the Education of Girls, reprinted with extracts from the evidence and a preface* (1869).

20. Despite efforts to recruit 'ladies' to elementary schoolteaching and nursing, these occupations attracted mainly women from the working and lower-middle classes; see F. Widdowson, *Going Up into the Next Class. Women and Elementary Teacher Training 1840-1914* (1980); F.B. Smith, *Florence Nightingale, Reputation and Power* (1982), pp.165-6.

21. *Intellectual Education and its Influence on the Character and Happiness of Women* (1858; second edition, 1862).

22. Frances Power Cobbe (1822-1904), journalist, was a member of the Langham Place set and a prominent campaigner for women's rights and against vivisection. Her paper of 1862 won the backing of the NAPSS for the opening of university-level examinations to women although it was ridiculed in the London daily press; B. Stephen, *Emily Davies*, p.82.

23. In 'Secondary Instruction as Relating to Girls'.

24. 'Family Chronicle', f.479.

25. F.A. Mumby, *Publishing and Bookselling. A History from the Earliest Times to the Present Day* (1930). pp.321-2.

26. Particularly Harriet Martineau (1802-1876), whose article on 'Female Industry' in the *Edinburgh Review* in 1859 had prompted the formation of the S.P.E.W.: O. Banks, *The Biographical Dictionary of British Feminism*, vol.i (1985), p.125.

27. Mrs. Grote to E. Davies, July 29, 1866, 'Family Chronicle', f.482.

28. Among them, B. Bodichon, *Women and Work* (1857), B.R. Parkes, *Essays on Women's Work* (1865) and numerous articles in the *English Woman's Journal*, analysed in Rendall, '"A Moral Engine?"'. Most of

Emily Davies' earlier writings are included in *Thoughts on Some Questions Relating to Women.*

29. H. Taylor to E. Davies, 18 June, 1866, 'Family Chronicle', ff.480-1.

30. *Westminster Review*, (lxxxvi), 1866, pp.487-9.

31. *Pall Mall Gazette*, 14 September 1866, p.833.

32. *Spectator*, 7 July 1866. pp.751-2.

33. See J.N. Burstyn, *Victorian Education and the Ideal of Womanhood* (1980).

34. Emily Davies' phrase, in her evidence to the Schools' Inquiry Commission; ed. Beale, *Reports*, p.187.

35. *Saturday Review*, vol.21, June 16 1866, pp.715-6, 'Women's Rights'.

36. J. Roach, *Public Examinations in England 1850-1900* (Cambridge, 1971), pp.103-136.

37. S. Delamont, 'The Contradictions in Ladies' Education', in Delamont and Duffin, *The Nineteenth Century Woman.*

38. See M. Vicinus, *Independent Women. Work and Community for Single Women, 1850-1920* (1985), pp.121-162.

39. J. Howarth and M. Curthoys, 'Gender, curriculum and career: a case study of women university students in England before 1914', in P. Summerfield (ed).,

Women, Education and the Professions (History of
Education Society Occasional Publication No.8, 1987).

40. *Manchester Guardian*, 25 March 1927.

41. B. Stephen, *Girton College, 1869-1932* (Cambridge,
1933), p.37.

42. Women were admitted to titular degrees in 1923
but to the M.A. only in 1984; see R. McWilliams
Tullberg, *Women at Cambridge. A Men's University –
though of a Mixed Type* (1975). An account of the more
pragmatic campaign which won Oxford women degrees
in 1920 is given in A.M.A.H. Rogers, *Degrees by
Degrees* (Oxford, 1938).

43. A term applied to her by Richard Hutton, editor of
the *Spectator* and a lecturer at Bedford College; R.H.
Hutton to E. Davies, 4 June 1866. 'I wonder you can
use such an impolite word' was Miss Davies' response.
'Family Chronicle' ff.462-8.

44. See M.C. Bradbrook, *Barbara Bodichon, George
Eliot and the Limits of Feminism* (Oxford, 1975).

45. E. Davies to H.R. Tomkinson, 14 November 1865,
'Family Chronicle', f.442.

46. G. Sutherland, 'The movement for the higher
education of women; its social and intellectual context',
in P.J. Waller (ed.), *Political and Social Change in
Modern Britain: Essays Presented to A.F. Thompson*
(1987), p.91.

THE HIGHER EDUCATION

OF WOMEN

CHAPTER I.

INTRODUCTORY.

IN any inquiry of a practical nature, intended to lead to some definite course of action, it is obviously necessary to start with a tolerably clear idea of the end in view—the object for which it is proposed to provide. In the case of education, definitions more or less satisfactory have already so

often been given, that it might seem
superfluous to go into the question again.
As · a matter of practice, however, it is
found that, when it is attempted to apply
the received definitions of the general objects of education to the case of women,
they are usually questioned or modified,
if not altogether set aside.   When, for
instance, Mr Maurice[1] tells us that 'the
end of education itself is, as it has always
been considered, to form a nation of living, orderly men,' the definition will be
accepted, with the tacit reservation that
it applies only to men, in the exclusive
sense of the word, and has nothing to do
with the education of women.   Again,
when Milton, in his treatise on Education,
lays down that the end of learning is 'to

repair the ruin of our first parents by re-
gaining to know God aright, and out of
that knowledge to love Him, to imitate
Him, to be like Him,' the language might
be taken in a general sense ; and when he
goes on to define a complete and generous
education as 'that which fits a man to
perform justly, skilfully, and magnani-
mously all the offices, both private and
public, of peace and war,' the words
might still, perhaps, bear a common in-
terpretation ; but as soon as he comes to
describing in detail, 'how all this may
be done between twelve and one-and-
twenty,' it becomes evident that he is
thinking of boys only.[2] In the most
recent writers, the tendency to regard
general theories of education as applying

exclusively to that of men, is quite as strongly marked.

It seems, therefore, that in attempting to treat of female education, it is necessary once more to ask what we are aiming at, and to obtain, if possible, a clear understanding and agreement as to the end in view. What ought the educators of girls to be trying to make of them? What is the ideal towards which they ought to direct their efforts, the end to be desired as the result of their labours?

To these questions we shall probably receive one or other of two answers. Many persons will reply, without hesitation, that the one object to be aimed at, the ideal to be striven after, in the education of women, is to make good wives and mothers. And the answer is a reasonable one, so far as it goes, and with explanations. Clearly, no education would be good which did not tend to make good wives and mothers; and that which produces the best wives and mothers is likely to be the best possible education. But, having made this admission, it is necessary to point out that an education of which the aim is thus limited, is likely to fail in that aim. That this is so will appear when the definition is transferred to the education of men. It will be admitted that a system of education which should produce bad husbands and fathers would prove itself to be bad; and an education which produces the best husbands and fathers is likely to be in all

respects the best; because the best man
in any capacity must be the man who
can measure most accurately the proportion of all his duties and claims, giving
to each its due share of his time and
energy. A man will not be the better
husband and father for neglecting his
obligations as a citizen, or as a man of
business. Nor will a woman be the
better wife or mother through ignorance
or disregard of other responsibilities.
There is, indeed, a view of male education which, having worldly advancement
for its ultimate object, regards it exclusively as a means of acquiring professional dexterity; but such a conception
of the purposes of education—however
legitimate, in a limited and subordinate

sense — when elevated into the position of the final goal, must be looked upon rather as a lapse from a higher standard, than as a principle deliberately maintained by any high-minded and thoughtful person. In disinterested schemes of male education, it is usually assumed, as a matter of course, that the great object is to make the best of a man in every respect, leaving him to adapt himself to specific relations, according to the state of life into which it shall please God to call him.

A similar idea seems to underlie the other, and more comprehensive reply, which will probably be given to our inquiry, namely, that the object of female education is to produce women of the

best and highest type, not limited by
exclusive regard to any specific functions
hereafter to be discharged by them. This
answer at once brings down upon us
the terrible question, What *is* the best
and highest type of woman? And as
this question lies at the root of the
whole matter, it cannot be passed by.
Many people, indeed, talk as if it was
a matter on which the world had long
since made up its mind, and which might
be assumed to be already decided. But
when we ask what it is that the world
has decided, it is difficult to obtain anything like a clear and unanimous answer.
The ideal differs not only among different
races, and in different ages, but most
widely in our own country, and in

modern times. Unanimity is scarcely to be found in any class of writers or thinkers, though on this point, of all others, some sort of agreement, at least between parents and teachers, would seem to be most essential. It may perhaps be of service, as a step towards a mutual understanding, to examine, though necessarily in a very imperfect and cursory manner, some of the most commonly received notions current on the subject.

CHAPTER II.

IDEALS.

THERE is a theory afloat, extensively prevalent, and probably influencing many persons who have never stated it definitely to themselves, that the human ideal is composed of two elements, the male and the female, each requiring the other as its complement; and that the realisation of this ideal is to be found in no single human

being, man or woman, but in the union
of individuals by marriage, or by some
sort of vague marriage of the whole race.
The conception of character which rests
on the broad basis of a common human-
ity falls into the background, and there
is substituted for it a dual theory, with
distinctly different forms of male and
female excellence. Persons who take
this view are naturally governed by
it in their conceptions of what women
ought to be. Having framed a more
or less definite idea of the masculine
character, in constructing the feminine
helpmeet they look out, if not for the
directly opposite, for what they would
call the complementary qualities, and the
conclusion quickly follows, that whatever

is manly must be unwomanly, and *vice
versâ*. The advocates of this view usually
hold in connexion with it certain doctrines, such as, that the man is intended
for the world, woman for the home;
man's strength is in the head, woman's
in the heart; the man's function is to
protect, woman's to soothe and comfort;
men must work, and women must weep:
everywhere we are to have a sharply
marked division, often honestly mistaken
for the highest and most real communion.[3]
Closely connected with these separatist
doctrines is the double moral code, with
its masculine and feminine virtues, and
its separate law of duty and honour for
either sex.

The general acceptance of the theory

is not surprising. It gratifies the logical instinct; and many persons, hastily taking for granted that it is the only conception of the relations between men and women which recognises real distinctions, assume it to be the only one which satisfies the craving of the æsthetic sense for harmony and fitness. Unfortunately it is not workable. We make the world even more puzzling than it is by nature, when we shut our eyes to the facts of daily life; and we know, as a fact, that women have a part in the world, and that men are by no means ciphers in the home circle—we know that a man who should be all head would be as monstrous an anomaly as a woman all heart—that men require the protection of law, and

women are not so uniformly prosperous
as to be independent of comfort and
consolation—men have no monopoly of
working, nor women of weeping. The
sort of distinction it is attempted to
establish, though not without an element
of truth when rightly understood, is for
the most part artificial, plausible in ap-
pearance, but breaking down under the
test of experience. When overstrained,
and made the foundation of a divided
moral code, it is misleading in proportion
to its attractiveness.

Happily this theory, though deeply and
widely and most subtilely influential, is
not completely dominant. People who go
to church, and who read their Bibles, are
perpetually reminded of one type and

exemplar, one moral law. The theory of education of our English Church recognises no distinction of sex. The baptized child is signed with the sign of the cross, 'in token that hereafter he—or she—shall not be ashamed to confess the faith of Christ crucified, and manfully to fight under His banner, against sin, the world, and the devil ; and to continue Christ's faithful soldier and servant to his—or her—life's end.' The sponsors are charged to provide that the child be 'virtuously brought up to lead a godly and a Christian life, remembering always that baptism doth represent unto us our profession, which is to follow the example of our Saviour Christ, and to be made like unto Him.' The catechism in which the child is to be

instructed, gives no hint of separate standards of duty. The catechumens are
required to give an account of their duty
towards God and towards their neighbour. The latter supplies a statement
of social obligations, in which, if any-
where, we should surely find a distinction
laid down between the duties of men and
those of women. But no such distinction
appears. In Confirmation, the children,
having come to years of discretion, ratify
and confirm in their own persons what has
gone before, still without a hint of diver-
gent duties. The same principle appears
in the formularies of the Scotch Church.
The Shorter Catechism teaches that 'God
created man, male and female, after His
own image, in knowledge, righteousness,

and holiness, with dominion over the creatures;' and that 'man's chief end is to glorify God, and to enjoy Him for ever.'

Here all is clear and consistent. Thoroughly to carry out the Christian theory would no doubt lead to some startling consequences; but the theory itself is intelligible and workable. Can the same be said of any other of the standards or tests by which educators might shape their work? The only intelligible principle on which modern writers show anything like unanimity, is that women are intended to supply, and ought to be made, something which men want. What that may be, it is not easy to discover. We are met at the outset by a difficulty as to the nature of the want. We may want what we

like, or we may want what will do us
good — and the two qualities are not
always combined.   Usually, however, it
is taken for granted that, in this case,
men like what is good for them ; and it
only remains, therefore, to be ascertained
what it is that they like.

There is no lack of evidence.   English
literature is full of oracular information
on the subject.   Mr Anthony Trollope[4]
says : 'We like women to be timid.'
Mr Helps[5] complains that ' women are
not taught to be courageous.   Indeed, to
some persons courage may seem as un-
necessary for women as Latin and Greek.
Yet there are few things that would tend
to make women happier in themselves,
and more acceptable to those with whom

they live, than courage. . . . So far from courage being unfeminine, there is a peculiar grace and dignity in those beings who have little active power of attack or defence, passing through danger with a moral courage which is equal to that of the strongest.'

Abundance of applause has been bestowed upon Miss Nightingale and the other 'heroines of the Crimea,' whose enterprise certainly required no small share of masculine resolution.[6] On the other hand, a writer on the position of women confesses to ' an admiration for the commonplace, unambitious kind of old maid, who is content to do good in her own neighbourhood, and among the few persons whom she really knows—who takes

a lively interest in the welfare of her
nephews and nieces, and who regales herself occasionally with tea and gossip.'

One writer tells us that there are things
for which women are exclusively fitted.
' In the first place, women have the power
of pleasing. Accomplishments are cultivated as instrumental to the successful
exercise of this power, and therefore are
not to be rejected on the ground that they
waste the time that might be given to
mathematics. The common sense of the
world has long ago settled that men are
to be pleased, and women are to please.
Accordingly women acquire an agreeable
expertness at the piano, and view the
acquisition as a solemn duty.' Another,
in answer to the question, what ought all

young ladies to learn, says, 'Accomplishments are quite a secondary matter. If men do not get tired of the songs, they soon get tired of the singer, if she can do nothing but sing. What is really wanted in a woman is, that she should be a permanently pleasant companion. So far as education can give or enhance pleasantness, it does so by making the view of life wide, the wit ready, the faculty of comprehension vivid.'

One authority, delightfully contented with things as they are, assures us that, 'humanly speaking, the best sort of British young lady is all that a woman can be expected to be—civil, intelligent, enthusiastic, decorous, and, as a rule, prettier than in any other country. We are per-

fectly satisfied with what we have got.' Another, less happily constituted, asserts that
'all good judges and good teachers lament
the present system of girls' education. It
is all cramming, and with such very poor
results. After all is over, girls know very
little and care about less. Most girls are
decidedly stupid, and what good can
cramming of the most barren and repul-
sive kind do to stupid girls ? We should
consider what we want women to be.
That they should be trained to be good
and generous is by far the first thing. . . .
The next thing is that they should be well-
mannered and healthy. The third requisite is, that they should know how to
express themselves—should have a right
standard in judging books and men, and

public and private life. . . . The fourth
requisite is, that they should know how to
bear rule in a household. . . . These are all
the essentials.'

Another view is, that a woman should
be ' a gentle tyrant, capricious indeed, yet
generous and kindhearted withal, varying
in mood, now clouded, now serene, though
given less to tears than laughter, and
bright with gleams of hopeful sunshine
like the spring. She should be no dunce,
no ignoramus, this enviable woman ; she
should not have stopped in her education
when the governess's back was turned, nor
hold that to play Mr Chappell's music
creditably is the one aim and end of all
instruction ; she should know enough to
take her part in topics of general conver-

sation, to read the *Times* with interest, and talk about the leading article without a yawn; she should be fond enough of learning to find that her leisure seldom hangs heavy on her hands; and if (though it is almost too much to expect) she has sufficient patience with the process of induction to be able to reason on any subject for two minutes together without jumping to a conclusion either way, we may well congratulate ourselves on having drawn the great prize in the lottery of life.' Mr Coventry Patmore seems to prefer that the gentle tyranny and the capriciousness should be on the other side.

'He who toils all day,
And comes home hungry, tired or cold,
And feels 'twould do him good to scold

His wife a little, let him trust
Her love, and boldly be unjust,
And not care till she cries! How prove
In any other way his love
Till soothed in mind by meat and rest?
If, after that, she's well caress'd,
And told how good she is to bear
His humour, fortune makes it fair.
Women like men to be like men,
That is, at least, just now and then!'[7]

The wife is here represented as rejoicing in her husband's ill-temper, as affording her an opportunity of dispelling it by soothing arts, a practical illustration, it may be observed, of the complementary theory, the woman's patience actually demanding a man's sulkiness to practise upon. Contrast Mr Patmore's 'Jane' with Mr Tennyson's 'Isabel.'

'Eyes not down-dropt nor over-bright, but fed
With the clear-pointed flame of chastity,

Clear, without heat, undying, tended by
Pure vestal thoughts in the translucent fane
Of her still spirit; locks not wide-dispread,
Madonna-wise on either side her head;
Sweet lips whereon perpetually did reign
The summer calm of golden charity,
Were fixed shadows of thy fixed mood,
   Revered Isabel, the crown and head,
The stately flower of female fortitude,
    Of perfect wifehood and pure lowlihead.

'The intuitive decision of a bright
And thorough-edged intellect to part
   Error from crime; a prudence to withhold;
   The laws of marriage character'd in gold
Upon the blanched tablets of her heart;
A love still burning upward, giving light
To read those laws; an accent very low
In blandishment, but a most silver flow
   Of subtle-paced counsel in distress,
Right to the heart and brain, though undescried,
   Winning its way with extreme gentleness
Through all the outworks of suspicious pride;
A courage to endure and to obey;
A hate of gossip parlance, and of sway,
Crown'd Isabel, through all her placid life,
The queen of marriage, a most perfect wife.' [8]

The self-defence which Shakespeare puts
into the mouth of Queen Katherine de-
scribes a different type :—

> 'Heaven witness
> I have been to you a true and humble wife,
> At all times to your will conformable ;
> Ever in fear to kindle your dislike,
> Yea, subject to your countenance ; glad or sorry,
> As I saw it incline.   When was the hour
> I ever contradicted your desire,
> Or made it not mine too ? or which of your friends
> Have I not strove to love, although I knew
> He were mine enemy ? what friend of mine
> That had to him derived your anger, did I
> Continue in my liking ? nay, gave notice
> He was from thence discharged ?' [9]

This picture of trembling devotion, of
' distrust qualified by fear,' appears in a
selection called ' Beautiful Poetry,' under
the heading 'A True Wife.'   But this
kind of wife would be positively disliked
by some husbands.   It has been said that

'perhaps—such is masculine nature—a wife with more knowledge, more fixity of thought, and more general mental power than one's-self might be "a blessing in disguise." But one who is goose enough to sympathise at random on subjects of which she knows little or nothing, because it is "feminine" to do so, is a nuisance *not* in disguise. . . . For our own part, we would just as soon have the sympathy of a chameleon as that of a woman who lives completely in particulars, and is quite destitute of power to appreciate a universal principle.'

These are but a few samples, culled almost at random from the mass of contradictory evidence to be found in English literature. Conceive a governess or school-

mistress, duly impressed with the obligation
of training her pupils to be accomplished
pleasers of men, and trying to fashion for
them a model out of such materials! Must
not the result be simply blank despair?
The same conclusion might be reached by
a shorter process. Men are supposed to
marry the sort of women they like. But
looking upon the infinite variety of wives
to be met with in society, could any one
generalise from them a model wife, who
might serve as a pattern to educators?
Would any man wish for a wife so mo-
delled? Might it not be as well to abandon this distracting theory—to discard the
shifting standard of opinion, and to fall
back upon the old doctrine which teaches
educators to seek in every human soul for

that divine image which it is their work
to call out and to develope?

The educational question depends, as
we have seen, on the larger question of
women's place in the social order. Are
they to be regarded, and to regard themselves, primarily as children of God, members of Christ, and heirs of the kingdom of
heaven, and, secondarily, as wives, mothers,
daughters, sisters? or are the family relationships to overshadow the divine and
the social, and to be made the basis of a
special moral code, applying to women
only? According to the first view, all
human duties—everything that is lovely
and of good report—all moral virtues and
all Christian graces are inculcated and
enforced by the highest sanctions. An

ascetic contempt for wifely and motherly and daughterly ties is no part of the Christian ideal. But the view which teaches women to think of family claims as embracing their whole duty—which bids them choose to serve man rather than God—sets before them a standard of obligation which, in proportion as it is exclusively adhered to, vitiates not their lives only, but those of the men on whom their influence might be of a far different sort. That such a theory is radically inconsistent with the divine order might easily be shown. That its action on society is profoundly demoralising is a lesson taught by mournful experience.

CHAPTER III.

THINGS AS THEY ARE.

WHETHER it is owing to the prevailing confusion of ideas as to the objects of female education, or to whatever cause it may be attributed, there can be little doubt that the thing itself is held in slight esteem. No one indeed would go so far as to say that it is not worth while to educate girls at all. *Some* education is held to be indispensable, but how much is an open question ; and the general indifference operates in the way of continually postponing it to other claims, and, above all, in shortening the time allotted to systematic instruction and discipline. Parents are ready to make sacrifices to secure a tolerably good and complete education for their sons ; they do not consider it necessary to do the same for their daughters. Or perhaps it would be putting it more fairly to say, that a very brief and attenuated course of instruction, beginning late and ending early, is believed to constitute a good and complete education for a woman.

It is usually assumed that when a boy's school education has once begun, which it does at a very early age, it is to go on

steadily till he is a man. A boy who leaves
school at sixteen or eighteen, either enters
upon some technical course of training for
a business or profession, or he passes on to
the University, and from thence to active
work of some sort or other. In other
words, he is *in statu pupillari* until general education and professional instruction
are superseded by the larger education
supplied by the business of life. In the
education of girls no such regular order
appears. A very usual course seems to
be for girls to spend their early years in a
haphazard kind of way, either at home,
or in not very regular attendance at an
inferior school; after which they are sent
for a year or two to a school or college to
finish. The heads of schools complain

with one voice that they are called upon
to 'finish' what has never been begun,
and that to attempt to give anything like
a sound education, in the short time at
their disposal, is perfectly hopeless. But,
to take the most favourable case,—that of
a girl so well prepared that she is able to
make good use of the teaching provided in
a first-rate school,—just at the moment
when she is making real, substantial progress, she is taken away. At sixteen,
seventeen, or eighteen, as the case may be,
her education comes to an abrupt pause.
When she marries, it may be said to begin
again; but between leaving school and
marriage there is usually an interval of at
least three or four years, if not a much
longer period. These years a youth

spends, as has been before said, in preparation for his future career. In the case
of girls, no such preparation seems to be
considered necessary.

Is this reasonable? Apart from immediate pecuniary necessity, is it desirable
that the regular education of women
should be considered as finished at the
age of eighteen? If we are to take the
almost universal practice as an answer, it
is a very decided affirmative. Even girls
whose parents must be fully aware that
they will eventually have to maintain themselves, seldom receive any adequate training for their future work. Those whose
fathers intend to provide for them, are still
less likely to be supposed to want any
further education after they leave school.

THINGS AS THEY ARE.   37

So fixed and wide-spread a custom must have had, at some time or other, even if it has not now, a meaning and a justification. And this may perhaps be found in the fact that our mothers and our grandmothers were accustomed to undergo at home, after leaving school, what was in fact an apprenticeship to household management. It seems indeed at one time to have been customary to apprentice girls of what we now call the middle class, to trades,—as we find George Herbert urging his Country Parson not to put his children 'into vain trades and unbefitting the reverence of their father's calling, such as are taverns for men and lacemaking for women,'[10]—but even where there was no apprenticeship to a specific business, the round of household labours would supply a very considerable variety of useful occupation. An active part in these labours would naturally devolve upon the daughters of the house, who would thus be forming habits of industry and order invaluable in after life.

Probably a great many fathers, profoundly ignorant as they are of the lives of women, cherish a vague imagination that the same kind of thing is going on still. If Providence should at any time lead them to spend a week in the society of their daughters, under ordinary circumstances—not when illness has altered the usual current of affairs—they would find that this is very far from being the case. That great male public, which

spends its days in chambers and offices
and shops, knows little of what is going
on at home. Writers in newspapers and
magazines are fond of talking about the
nursery, as if every household contained
a never-ending supply of young children,
on whom the grown-up daughters might
be practising the art of bringing up.
Others have a great deal to say about
the kitchen, assuming it to be desirable
that the ladies of the house should super-
sede, or at least assist, the cook. In that
case, where there is a mother with two or
three daughters, we should have four or
five cooks. The undesirableness of such
a multiplication of artists need scarcely
be pointed out.* Needlework, again,

* As this pursuit is sometimes recommended with

occupies a much larger space in the imagination of writers than it does in practical life.   Except in families where there are children, there is very little plain needlework to be done, and what there is, many people make a point of giving out, on the ground that it is better to pay a half-starved needlewoman for work done, than to give her the money in the form of alms.

apparent seriousness, it may be as well to point out to the uninitiated, that if mistresses are to do the cooking, masters must dine alone.   Dinners cannot be cooked an hour beforehand, and left to serve themselves up.   In this, as in other arts, the finishing touches are among the most important.   This does not mean, of course, that a mistress may not give directions and occasional help, or that it may not be a very good thing for girls to lend a hand, now and then, by way of learning to cook.   That is a different thing from regularly spending a considerable part of their daily lives in the kitchen.

Having mentioned needlework, cookery, and the care of children, we seem to have come to an end of the household work in which ladies are supposed to take part. If young women of eighteen and upwards are learning anything in their daily life at home, it must be something beside and beyond the acquirement of dexterity in ordinary domestic arts.

Many fathers, however, are no doubt aware that their daughters have very little to do. But that seems to them anything but a hardship. They wish they had a little less to do themselves, and can imagine all sorts of interesting pursuits to which they would betake themselves if only they had a little more leisure. Ladies, it may be said, have their choice, and they must evidently prefer idleness, or they would find something to do. If this means that half-educated young women do not choose steady work when they have no inducement whatever to overcome natural indolence, it is no doubt true. Women are not stronger - minded than men, and a commonplace young woman can no more work steadily without motive or discipline than a commonplace young man. It has been remarked that 'the active, voluntary part of man is very small, and if it were not economised by a sleepy kind of habit, its results would be null. We could not do every day out of our own heads all we have to do. We should accomplish nothing ; for all our energies would be frittered away in minor

attempts at petty improvement.' The case
of young women could scarcely have been
better stated.   Every day they have to do
out of their own heads nearly all that they
have to do.   They accomplish little ; for
their energies are frittered away in minor
attempts at petty improvement.

How true this is, the friends and coun-
sellors of girls could abundantly testify.
There is no point on which schoolmistresses
are more unanimous and more emphatic
than on the difficulty of knowing what to
do with girls after leaving school.   People
who have not been brought into intimate
converse with young women have little
idea of the extent to which they suffer
from perplexities of conscience.   ' The
discontent of the modern girl ' is not mere

idle self-torture. Busy men and women
—and people with disciplined minds—can
only, by a certain strain of the imagination, conceive the situation. If they at all
entered into it, they could not have the
heart to talk as they do. For the case of
the modern girl is peculiarly hard in this,
that she has fallen upon an age in which
idleness is accounted disgraceful. The
social atmosphere rings with exhortations
to act, act in the living present. Everywhere we hear that true happiness is to be
found in work—that there can be no leisure without toil—that people who do
nothing are unfruitful fig-trees which
cumber the ground. And in this atmosphere the modern girl lives and breathes.

She is not a stone, and she does not live underground. She hears people talk—she listens to sermons—she reads books. And in her reading she comes across such passages as the following :—

'It is a real pleasure to me to find that you are taking steadily to a profession, without which I scarcely see how a man can live honestly. That is, I use the term "profession" in rather a large sense, not as simply denoting certain callings which a man follows for his maintenance, but rather a definite field of duty, which the nobleman has as much as the tailor, but which he has not, who having an income large enough to keep him from starving, hangs about upon life, merely following his own caprices and fancies; *quod factu pessimum est.'* *

Or again :—

' N'est-il pas vrai que la fadeur de la vie est à la fois le grand malheur et le grand danger ?   Il y a une douzaine d'années, un orateur s'écriait à la tribune : " La France s'ennuie."   Et moi je dis : L'humanité s'ennuie, et son ennui ne date ni d'aujourd'hui ni d'hier, quoique peut-être il n'ait jamais été plus visible qu'en ce moment.   Sans la poursuite d'un but idéal, toute vie devient inevitablement insipide, même jusqu'au dégout.   Or, comptez parmi vos connaissances les personnes qui poursuivent un but élevé.   Beaucoup

* Letter to Dr Greenhill, an old pupil, in ' Life of Dr Arnold,' p. 392.

vivent sans savoir pourquoi, uniquement,
je pense, parce que chaque matin ramène
le soleil. Que de femmes, si vous exceptez
les mères qui se donnent à leur famille,
que de femmes, hélas, dont la vie se passe
entière dans de futiles occupations, ou dans
des conversations plus futiles encore ! Et
l'on s'étonne que, rongées d'ennui, elles
recherchent avec frénésie toutes les dis-
tractions imaginables ! Elles accusent la
monotonie de leur existence d'être la cause
de ce vague malaise ; la vraie cause est
ailleurs, elle est dans la fadeur intolérable,
non d'une vie dépourvue d'événements et
d'aventures, mais d'une vie dont on n'en-
trevoit pas la raison ni le but. On se
sent vivre sans qu'on y soit pour quelque
chose, et cette vie inconsciente, inutile,

absurde, inspire un mécontentement trop
fondé.'*

Such things the modern girl reads, and
every word is confirmed by her own experience.   With   the   practical   English
mind, which she has inherited from her
father, she applies it all to herself.   She
seeks for counsel, and she finds it.   She
is bidden to 'look around her' — to do
the duty that lies nearest—to teach in
the schools, or visit the poor—to take up
a pursuit—to lay down a course of study
and stick to it.   She looks around her,
and sees no particular call to active exertion.   The duties that lie in the way
are swallowed up by an energetic mother
or elder sister ; very possibly she has no

* Sermons par T. Colani.—*Deuxième Recueil*, p. 293.

vocation for philanthropy—and the most devoted philanthropists are the most urgent in warning off people who lack the vocation—or she lives in a village where the children are better taught than she could teach them, and the poor are already too much visited by the clergyman's family ; she feels no sort of impulse to take up any particular pursuit, or to follow out a course of study ; and so long as she is quiet and amiable, and does not get out of health, nobody wants her to do anything. Her relations and friends— her world—are quite satisfied that she should ' hang about upon life, merely following her own'—or their own—' caprices and fancies.' The advice given, so easy to offer, so hard to follow, pre-

supposes exactly what is wanting, a
formed and disciplined character, able to
stand alone, and to follow steadily a
predetermined course, without fear of
punishment, or hope of reward. Ought
we to wonder if, in the great majority of
cases, girls let themselves go drifting
down the stream, despising themselves,
but listlessly yielding to what seems to be
their fate ?

An appeal to natural guides is most
often either summarily dismissed, or received with reproachful astonishment. It
is considered a just cause for surprise and
disappointment, that well brought up
girls, surrounded with all the comforts of
home, should have a wish or a thought
extending beyond its precincts. And,

perhaps, it is only natural that parents
should be slow to encourage their
daughters in aspirations after any duties
and interests besides those of ministering
to their comfort and pleasure. In taking
for granted that this is the only object,
other than that of marriage, for which
women were created, they are but adopt-
ing the received sentiment of society. No
doubt, too, they honestly believe that, in
keeping their daughters to themselves till
they marry, they are doing the best thing
for them, as well as pleasing themselves.
If the daughters take a different view,
parents think it is because they are young
and inexperienced, and incompetent to
judge. The fact is, it is the parents
who are inexperienced. Their youth was

different in a hundred ways from the youth of this generation; and the experience of thirty years ago is far from being infallible in dealing with the difficulties and perplexities of the present. No doubt young people are ignorant, and want guidance. But they should be helped and advised, not silenced. Parents take upon themselves a heavy responsibility when they hastily crush the longing after a larger and more purposeful life.

That such an impulse is worthy of respect can scarcely be denied. The existence of capacities is in itself an indication that they are intended for some good purpose. Conscious power is not a burden, to be borne with patience, but a gift, for the due use of which the pos-

sessor rightly feels accountable. To have
a soul which can be satisfied with vanities
is not eminently virtuous and Christian,
but the reverse. To be awake to responsibilities, sensitive in conscience, quickly
responsive to all kindling influences, is a
sign that education has, so far, done a
good work. A flowing river is no doubt
more troublesome to manage than a tran-
quil pool ; but pools, if let alone too long,
are apt to become noxious, as well as
useless. The current may require to be
wisely directed ; but that there should
be a current of being, wanting to set
itself somewhere, is surely a cause for
thankful rejoicing. It is an unfortu-
nate misunderstanding of the true state
of the case that makes parents sigh

over what might well be their happiness and pride : one more exemplification of the sluggishness which hates nothing so bitterly as to be called upon to think—to consider a new idea—perhaps to go farther, and take a step out of the beaten track. It is much easier, no doubt, to say to a daughter who comes to you with her original notions—' My dear child, put it out of your head directly; it cannot be thought of for a moment'—than it would be to hear her patiently, to consider how far her crude ideas are practicable, to help her, so far as may be, in carrying them out.   And one ought not to wonder that the easiest course is the one most commonly chosen.   How far it may, or may not, be the duty of daughters to sacrifice their own wishes to the temporary pleasure of those to whom they owe so much, is a separate question. It is at least well for parents to know that, far more than they are at all aware of, it is felt to be a sacrifice, and that they must accept it as such, if at all.*

---

* 'M. de Parthenau would have been surprised had any one suggested that this peaceful life was less to the taste of his children than himself. Like so many excellent fathers, he sincerely believed that because it suited him, it must suit them. He had forgotten his own stormy youth, to find himself happy by his fireside, and it never occurred to him to ask, "Is my daughter happy?" So much the better, since he could have done nothing; and Thérèse was the last person to make him suspect that she was not perfectly satisfied. Yet, whoever had seen her, would have thought her destined for a wider sphere than that of the narrow world where she strove to be content. It had not always been so. Now, however, she stifled all the aspirations, the radiant visions which once haunted her, under the crowd of occupations which she found

The representation here given is, of course, not universally applicable. It is quite possible that in some senses, and to some persons, an apparently empty life may be easier, and even richer, than one of toil. There are people to whom the Happy Valley kind of life is by no

for herself. She silenced the cry of her intellect, and yet heard it always ; perhaps because she shunned as snares the natural outlets which presented themselves, refusing each rare opportunity of leaving home, lest she should return discontented ; and putting away books and pencils, that she might have no interests but those of her father and her poor dependents. It was an honest, mistaken effort to do right; and the confessor, who stood to her in the place of a conscience, approved it—nay, urged it on her. It was strange, this mute, ceaseless conflict, known only in its full extent to herself, and hidden under so monotonous and peaceful a life !'[11]*Sydonie's Dowry*, p. 24.

May not something like a counterpart of this mute, ceaseless conflict be hidden under many a monotonous and peaceful English life ?

means intolerable; and even earnest-
minded and conscientious girls, urged by
a strong sense of the heinousness of discontent, often manage to crush troublesome aspirations, and make themselves
happy. There is something undignified
in being miserable, without a just and
intelligible cause to show for it; and
many young women, capable of higher
things, accommodate themselves with a
considerable degree of cheerfulness to a
narrow and unsatisfying round of existence. Nor is it intended to represent
ladies as habitually doing nothing. On
the contrary, they have many resources.
Among them are various arts and handi-
crafts, gardening, letter-writing, and much
reading. Of these, the last is perhaps the

most popular and the most delusive. A girl who is 'very fond of reading' is considered to be happily suited with never-failing occupation, and no thought is taken as to what is to come of her reading. On this subject, the observations of Miss Aikin, herself an experienced reader, are worth considering.[12] 'Continual reading,' she says, 'if desultory, and without a definite object, favours indolence, unsettles opinions, and of course enfeebles the mental and moral energies.' And Mr Robertson of Brighton,[13] speaking in reference to girls, remarks that they 'read too much, and think too little. I will answer for it that there are few girls of eighteen who have not read more books than I have. . . . That multifarious reading weakens the mind more than doing nothing; for it becomes a necessity at last, like smoking, and is an excuse for the mind to lie dormant, whilst thought is poured in, and runs through, a clear stream, over unproductive gravel, on which not even mosses grow. It is the idlest of all idlenesses, and leaves more of impotency than any other.'

The same might be said of all merely *dilettante* occupation. Its fault is simply that it *is dilettante*—literally a pastime. It may as well be done, if nothing else turns up, and that is all. And this drawback, belonging to nearly all the ordinary work of young women, they are by themselves unable to overcome. Of course, the case is partly in their own hands,

and those who are by nature abnormally
energetic, will make a career for themselves in spite of difficulties. Where the
inward impulse is irrepressible, it becomes
a lantern to the feet, and a lamp unto
the path, making the way of duty plain
and unmistakable. But for the few whose
course is thus illumined, there will be the
many hovering in uneasy doubt, their
consciences and intellects just lively
enough to make them restless and unhappy, not sufficiently clear in their
minds as to right and wrong, either
to be nerved for vigorous action, or
to accept contentedly the conventional
duty of quiescence. There must be
something wrong in social regulations
which make a demand for exceptional

wisdom and strength on the part of any particular class; and that such a demand is made upon average young women is sufficiently clear. What society says to them seems to be something to this effect. Either you have force enough to win a place in the world, in the face of heavy discouragement, or you have not. If you have, the discipline of the struggle is good for you; if you have not, you are not worth troubling about. Is not this a hard thing to say to commonplace girls, not professing to be better or stronger than their neighbours? Why should their task be made, by social and domestic arrangements, peculiarly and needlessly difficult? And why should it be taken for granted that, if they fail, they must be extraordinarily silly or self-in-dulgent?   More than any other class, at the same age, they are exempted from direction and control — liberally gifted with the kind of freedom enjoyed by the denizens of a village pound. Within their prescribed sphere, they may wander at will, and if they 'there small scope for action see,' it is explained to them that they must not 'for this give room to discontent;' nor let their time 'be spent in idly dreaming' how they might be

> ' More free
> From outward hindrance or impediment.
> For presently this hindrance thou shalt find
> That without which all goodness were a task
> So slight, that virtue never could grow strong.'

In reply to such admonitions they are

tempted to inquire what task, other than that of dreaming, is set before them— what virtue, always excepting that one virtue of passive submission, has any chance of growing strong under such conditions. The 'slow,' who sink into dull inertia, and the 'fast,' who get rid of their superfluous energy in silly extravagances, have alike the excuse, that at the moment when they need the support of a routine explained and justified by a reasonable purpose, discipline and stimulus are at once withdrawn, leaving in their place no external support beyond the trivial demands and restraints of conventional society.

It may seem that an exaggerated importance is here attached to the interval between school and marriage; and if the considerations brought forward had reference to this period only, the charge would be just. But rightly to estimate the value of these years, we must bear in mind that they are the spring-time of life —the season of blossom, on which the fruit of the future depends. It is then that an impress is given to character which lasts through life. Opportunities then thrown away or misused can scarcely be recovered in later years. And it has seemed necessary to dwell upon the existing tenour of young women's lives, because, in dealing with the question of extending the duration of female education, we must be largely influenced by our conception of the alternative involved in leaving things as they are. It has been said that the end of education is 'to form a nation of living, orderly men.'[14] If it has been shown that the course now pursued tends to make a large part of the nation inanimate and disorderly, a case would seem to be established for urging efforts at improvement.

CHAPTER IV.

THINGS AS THEY MIGHT BE.

SUPPOSING so much to be granted, it will be asked, What can be done? Clearly, girls cannot be kept at school indefinitely till they marry. When they leave school, say at eighteen, what are they to do next? The answer must chiefly depend on circumstances. Where the resources of the parents are such that there is a reasonable certainty of an abundant provision for the future, an education corresponding with that given by the universities to young men—in other words, 'the education of a lady,' considered irrespectively of any specific uses to which it may afterwards be turned—would appear to be the desideratum. And clearly 'the education of a lady' ought to mean the highest and the finest culture of the time. The accurate habits of thought and the intellectual polish by which the scholar is distinguished, ought to be no less carefully sought in the training of women than in that of men. This would be true, even if only for the sake of the charm which high culture gives to social intercourse, a charm attainable in no other way. But apart from this consideration, the duties of women of the higher class are such as to demand varied knowledge as well as a disciplined mind and character. Difficult cases in social ethics frequently arise, on which women are obliged to act and to guide the action of others. However incompetent they may be, they cannot escape the responsibility of judging and deciding. And though natural sagacity and the happy impulses of which we hear so much often come to their aid, prejudice and mistaken impulses ought also to be taken into the account as disturbing elements of a very misleading kind. In dealing with social difficulties, the value of a cultivated judgment, able to unravel entangled evidence, and to give due weight to a great variety

of conflicting considerations, would seem
to be obvious enough. It would be well
worth while to exchange the wonderful
unconscious instinct, by which women are
supposed to leap to right conclusions, no
one knows how, for the conscious power of
looking steadily and comprehensively at
the whole facts of a case, and thereupon
shaping a course of action, with a clear
conception of its probable issues.   Of
course, a merely literary education will
not give this power. Knowledge of the
world and of human nature, only to be
gained by observation and experience, go
farther than mere knowledge of books.
But the habit of impartiality and deliber-
ation—of surveying a wide field of thought
—and of penetrating, so far as human eye

can see, into the heart of things—which is
promoted by genuine study even of books
alone—tends to produce an attitude of
mind favourable for the consideration of
complicated questions of any sort.   A
comparison between the judgment of a
scholar and that of an uneducated man on
matters requiring delicate discrimination
and grasp of thought, shows the degree in
which the intellect may be fitted by training for tasks of this nature.   A large and
liberal culture is probably also the best
corrective of the tendency to take petty
views of things, and on this account is
especially to be desired for women on
whom it devolves to give the tone to
' society.'

How far it may be desirable or justifiable for women to take part in political affairs is a vexed question, into which it is the less necessary here to enter, inasmuch as it is evident that the same kind of intellectual training which forms the groundwork of the education of a statesman is needed for other purposes. Women who think at all can scarcely help thinking about the condition of the poor, and to arrive at sound conclusions on so vast a subject involves an acquaintance more or less complete with almost every consideration which comes within the range of the politician. Unpaid work, such as the management of hospitals, workhouses, prisons and reformatories, and charitable societies, naturally devolves upon the leisurely classes, and

offers a field in which cultivated women
may fitly labour. And the moment they
enter upon such work, or attempt in any
way to alleviate the sufferings of the poor,
they find that a strong, clear head is as
necessary as a warm heart. The problem
how to deal with pauperism—the very
same difficulty which has hitherto baffled
the wisest of our statesmen—meets them
at the threshold of their works. The
encouragement or discouragement of the
pauper spirit depends in a great degree on
the discretion of district visitors and other
charitable agents; and the women who act
as the almoners of the rich and the advisers
of the poor need for their difficult task something more than mere gushing benevo-
lence. Or to take national education. 'My

Lords' make codes, revise and re-revise them, and Members of Parliament exhaust themselves in debates upon them; but a large share of their practical working devolves upon the wives and daughters of the clergy, and other ladies. Similarly of sanitary reform, which now attracts much attention. Sanitary laws and regulations have been enacted, and no doubt with good effect, but boards of health and inspectors can do but little without the intelligent co-operation of the women, on whom it depends to enforce personal and household hygiene in every family. Many other social questions might be mentioned on which women are required to know and to act. It would, in fact, be difficult to point out any measure of domestic policy which has been brought before Parliament during the last few years, on which it is not as directly important that right opinions should be formed by women as by men.

The higher education already spoken of would serve as a preparation for literary work, and as a groundwork for more definite technical instruction in every department of art. And, lastly, an extended course of study is, above all things, necessary for those who are to undertake the office of teaching others. The incompleteness of the education of schoolmistresses and governesses is a drawback which no amount of intelligence and goodwill can enable them entirely to overcome. It is obvious that for those who have to impart knowledge the primary requisite is to possess it; and it is one of the great difficulties of female teachers that they are called upon to instruct others, while very inadequately instructed themselves. The more earnest and conscientious devote their leisure hours to continued study, and, no doubt, much may be done in this way; but it is at the cost of overwork, often involving the sacrifice of health, to say nothing of the disadvantages of working alone, without a teacher, often without good books, and without the wholesome stimulus of companionship.

These considerations lead up to the more distinctly professional side of the question, that which relates to the pur-

suit of any particular calling as a means
of maintenance.   Every one knows that
there are women, some even of the upper
class, who must earn their own living;
and this being admitted, it will scarcely
be disputed that they ought to be put
into the best way of doing it.   The thing
to find out seems to be what professions
are there, taking the word as including
business of all sorts, to which they might
betake themselves with a fair prospect of
success ? Perhaps we may gain some light
by looking into history, and seeing what
went on in earlier times, before the ad-
vance of science, with its infinite sub-
divisions of labour, had made it almost
impossible to carry on any profitable
pursuit within the precincts of home.

Confining ourselves, for the sake of brevity, to English history, we find among the ordinary avocations of women Medicine and Surgery, including the compounding and dispensing of drugs ; the service of the afflicted and distressed in mind, body, or estate ; farming ; marketing ; and a variety of domestic manufactures, too numerous to recite in detail.

Would the same pursuits, under regulations adapted to altered conditions, be proper for women now ? Among those which have been mentioned, that of Medicine appears peculiarly desirable, as affording scope for the exercise of the highest gifts, in a field in which women's close acquaintance with the details of domestic life would be a valuable adjunct.

The medical profession is now accessible to any competent woman who is able to defray the cost of instruction. The licence of the Court of Apothecaries, which constitutes a legal qualification for general practice, is given on passing the required examinations. There is no difficulty in the way of apprenticeship, and lectures and hospital practice are attainable, though at a higher cost to individual students, than would be incurred if the expense were divided among several. The objection often urged against the practice of medicine by women, that they have no confidence in each other, and that a medical woman would therefore find herself without patients, can only be conclusively answered by facts. *À priori*, there is some

reason to believe, that, always assuming
the education to be equally thorough and
equally well attested, the services of a
lady will be preferred; but till women
have full opportunity of choice, it is impossible to say positively what they will
choose. The experience of a few years
will decide. In the meantime, Miss Garrett's very remarkable success is at least
encouraging to other aspirants in the same
field.[15]

Closely allied to the practice of medicine are the functions of educated women
in ministering to the poor, the insane, and
the criminal. These services, so far as
they are paid, are now chiefly carried on
in workhouses, hospitals, reformatories,
and penitentiaries. The superintendence

of nurses and the offices of matron and
schoolmistress are in the hands of women,
and there seems room for further development in this direction.   It may be a question for consideration whether in some
cases it might not be desirable to substi-
tute the services of an educated Christian
lady for those of the chaplain.   The duties
of a workhouse chaplain are thus defined
by the Poor-Law Board :—[16]

' ART. 211. *Duties of the Chaplain.*

' The following shall be the duties of
the chaplain :—

' No. 1. To read prayers, and preach a
sermon to the paupers and other inmates
of the workhouse on every Sunday, and
on Good Friday and Christmas-day, unless

the guardians, with the consent of the
commissioners, may otherwise direct.

'No. 2. To examine the children, and
to catechise such as belong to the Church
of England, at least once in every month,
and to make a record of the same, and
state the dates of his attendance, the
general progress and condition of the children, and the moral and religious state of
the inmates generally, in a book to be kept
for that purpose, to be laid before the
guardians at their next ordinary meeting,
and to be termed "The Chaplain's Report."

'No. 3. To visit the sick paupers, and to
administer religious consolation to them in
the workhouse, at such periods as the guardians may appoint, and when applied to
for that purpose by the master or matron.'

The work laid out under the two last clauses might certainly be done as well, in some respects perhaps better, by a duly qualified lady; and on the face of it, there seems to be no particular reason why paupers should not attend their parish church and be visited by the clergyman like other parishioners. The desirableness of workhouse visiting by ladies has been much discussed, and is now beginning to be acknowledged. The presence of a lady in an official capacity might be still more valuable, both as being permanent and as waiving the difficulties which are so apt to come in the way of philanthropic inter-ference in state institutions. A lady appointed expressly by the guardians themselves could scarcely provoke jealousy, and her representations, based on thorough knowledge of the matter in hand, and modified by sympathy with the difficulties and scruples of authorities, as well as with the claims of the suffering, would be comparatively exempt from the charge of officiousness. That she would naturally gather round her such helpers as she might need in an unofficial capacity is an obvious advantage. The same observations would seem to be applicable to hospitals and prisons, and all public institutions where women are employed in a subordinate capacity. That the presence and the active influence of a lady, by whatever name she might be called, would be a valuable element, wherever the sick in mind or body are congregated together, is

generally admitted, though the theory has
not in England been acted upon to any
considerable extent.

Next in our enumeration comes the
business of farming. The social prejudice
against useful occupations of any sort, as
distinguished from those which are supposed to be ornamental, has here been
actively at work. The superintendence
of farming operations is still, however,
largely shared by women, especially in the
north of England. In commercial deal-
ings there is a good deal of work to be
done which could not, at any rate in our
present very imperfect state of civilisation,
be properly undertaken by women. There
are, however, branches of mercantile and
quasi-mercantile business, including that

profession of modern growth which has
been called 'management,'—in which wise
arrangements, carefully made, are all that
is required to make them suitable.   In
almost every kind of business, wholesale
and retail, the book-keeping and the correspondence might be very fitly carried
on by competent women.[17]

With regard to the manufactures which
now form so vast a portion of our national industry, a great revolution has
taken place, and it is here, above all, that
a re-adjustment of social and domestic
arrangements, involving some innovation
on conventional ideas and usages, seems
to be imperatively needed.   Down to a
comparatively recent period, every household was a workshop.   It is within the

present generation that the sewing-machine has laid hold of the last remaining implement of domestic manufacture. The home is no longer a manufactory. Spinning, weaving, knitting, sewing, all are gone, or going. What has become of the busy hands and brains? The hands are gone into factories, the brains are idle. We cannot call back the hands, and again set them to work in the domestic manufactory. Might it not be possible to bring them again under womanly influence, and at the same time find fit work for the brains, by introducing women of the employing class into factories? Might we not restore the old order of things, under which the payers of wages and the receivers of wages worked together, to the

mutual advantage of both—by replacing
women in the position of directors and
overlookers of female labour ? It is vain
to say that a factory is not a fit place for
a lady. If it is not, it ought to be made
so. If the moral atmosphere of a workshop is necessarily debasing, no human
being ought to be exposed to its influence.
But is it *necessarily* debasing ? Are ma-
chines in themselves demoralising ? What
is the moral difference between a spin-
ning-jenny and a distaff ? Are knitting-
needles refined, and knitting-machines
coarse ? Is there any reason, in the
nature of things, why the moral tone of
a factory should be less pure and elevating than that of the home ? Is it not
rather that we want, in our modern

workshops, the influence conveyed by
daily intercourse between women to
whom wealth has given the means of
culture and refinement, and the labourers
whom poverty obliges to work with their
hands, but who need not therefore part
with any essential feminine attribute ?
If, in all the works where women are
employed in the inferior departments, the
daughters of the masters were instructed
in the business, made so thoroughly con-
versant with it as to be able to take a
real part in its direction, two advantages
would be gained.   The higher class of
workers would acquire larger sympathies,
more living interests, increased aptitude
for affairs, and an exhilarating sense of
usefulness — of having a place in the

world from which they would be missed
if they were withdrawn from it. The
lower class would, on their part, be
elevated by the contact with a genuine
refinement, not too 'fine' to be useful.
They would see that a lady is a lady, not
in virtue of her costly dress and luxurious
habits, but in the gentleness, the truth-
fulness, and the sensitive sympathy, which
are among the most precious fruits of
high culture. And it can scarcely be
doubted that such an example, such an
ideal, brought within the immediate and
daily contemplation of women and girls
of the labouring class, would be more
effectual in rectifying their standard of
morals and refinement than any philanthropic agency, however well-intentioned

and judicious, which could be brought to bear from without. In some cases there might be difficulties in the way of teaching women the practical parts of a manufacture, but there can be few businesses in which some place might not be found for them. Even where female labourers are not employed in the lower departments — though there the case is the strongest—women might often take part in the direction, with great advantage to themselves, and at least without injury to any one else.

It appears, then, that a transference of the scene of action, and an accommodation of old principles and practices to new circumstances, is the task of the present generation, and the true answer to

the appeal of women for something to do.
The change proposed, so far from being a
departure from the old ways, is, in fact,
a recurrence to them. The advocates of
things as they are, are the innovators.
Those who sigh after things as they might
be, are the old-fashioned people, eager to
retain, with only such modifications as
advancing civilisation has made indispensable, all that is best in things as they
were.

CHAPTER V.

PROFESSIONAL AND DOMESTIC LIFE.

AN obvious rejoinder to the foregoing suggestions will at once
present itself. It will be said
that professions and business may be all
very well—may indeed be best—for single
women, but that sooner or later the great
majority marry, and any plan of life
which fails to recognise this contingency
is unpractical and absurd. This is most

true. We have to deal with facts; and it is a most important, though not the sole question, How would a higher education and professional training act upon family life? Home duties fall to the lot of almost every woman, and nothing which tends to incapacitate for the performance of them ought to be encouraged. Let us ask, then, what are the home duties of women as such, and what are the qualifications required for their discharge? And here we must remember that the claims involved in the conjugal and parental and filial relations are not special to women. They are not, indeed, to be disregarded in considering the bearing of a scheme of education; but in the discussion of the home duties of women *as such*, it is convenient to treat separately those which are not shared by men.

If we bring before our mind's eye the picture of an English home, we see that the household work is divided between the mistress and the servants. Where there are grown-up daughters, they sometimes help the mistress in her work, or the servants in theirs, but they have no distinct functions of their own. It appears, then, that in an inquiry relating to the upper and middle classes, the only home duties special to women which can come under review, are those of the mistress of the household. What are her functions? Those of government and administration. All housekeepers will agree that this is the work they have to

do, though they may not be accustomed
to call it by these names. The inexperienced mistress complains, not that she
does not know how to cook, or to sew,
or to keep the furniture in order—these
arts, if she wants them, can be quickly
acquired ; her perplexity is how to manage the servants. To draw the line between necessary subordination and vexa-
tious interference—to apportion to each
a fair share of work, and to see that the
work is done—to be liberal and conside-
rate without over-indulgence,—these are
duties requiring judgment, moderation,
method, decision, often no small share of
moral courage ; in other words, precisely
the same qualities which are wanted in
governing bodies of workpeople. In

administration also, it is obvious that, though on a different scale, the same sagacity, prudence, and foresight which would make a woman successful in business, would conduce to the economical management of domestic concerns.

The head of a household wants an ideal to work up to, and the governing and administrative power which will enable her to carry out her idea. Here, as elsewhere, motive is the primary requisite. A woman to whom huggermugger is intolerable will find means of escaping from it—if necessary, by the labour of her own hands—more often, perhaps, by the skilful direction of the labour of others. But one who has no inner sense of the beauty of order, to whom the rhythmic flow of a

well-governed household is an unmeaning
conception, or who lacks the gift of mas-
tery over details, may be cooking and
sewing and looking after things from
morning till night ; she may be anxiously
obedient to conventional regulations, rigid
in the observance of ceremonies unmeaning in themselves or unsuited to her position ; with all her striving, she will never
realise the vision of an ideal English
home.

It appears, then, that first, imagination, combined with a certain sensitiveness
of refinement, and secondly, the faculty
of government and administration, are
the qualifications chiefly necessary for
the performance of home duties. No
education can be relied upon as infallibly

securing these rare gifts; but it may be
assumed that extensive reading of the
best books tends to cultivate imagination
and refinement, and that a life of active
exertion tends to bring out the qualities
which go to make up the governing and
administrative faculty; and if so, a liberal
education and the pursuit of a profession
are perhaps, on the whole, the best training that the conditions of modern society
can supply for the special functions of
the mistress of a household.

It will, however, be pointed out by
practical people, that even supposing the
training to be good as regards domestic
life, parents will not throw away their
money on a costly preparation for a profession which is most likely to be aban-

doned in a few years ; and again, that the contingency of marriage is likely to act as a discouragement to girls, making them so languid in endeavour, that they would have small chance of success in a professional career.

To the last objection experience would not lead us to attach much weight. But supposing that, either through want of energy or perseverance, or from any other deficiency, women should take a low place in the professional ranks, what then ? The object of their education would have been, not to set them on a pinnacle of distinction, but to make them useful labourers ; and if this end were attained, society, at any rate, would have no reason to complain.

It is true, however, that fathers are likely to hesitate in spending money on what may seem a doubtful speculation as regards pecuniary returns. And if marriage necessarily involves the complete abandonment of a profession, the chances are somewhat against professional education as an investment of capital, though perhaps less so than would at first sight appear. Of course much depends on the amount of money which it is necessary to expend. To take the medical profession, as being, among those which women are likely to enter, the one in which the cost of training is probably the highest—it is a liberal computation to allow £500 as covering the cost of instruction over and above the personal expenses, which would be going on all the same whether a girl were being educated or not. Such a sum would, in three or four years of successful practice, be recovered, and any further earnings would be clear gain. No doubt, in cases of very early marriage, a part or even the whole of the sum expended would be sunk; and the result of giving women professions would probably be, on the whole, to encourage comparatively early marriage, partly by bringing persons of congenial tastes into mutual intercourse, and partly by rendering marriages possible which would otherwise be flagrantly imprudent. But supposing that a woman married a rich man before she had begun to practise, the loss of the sum mentioned could easily be spared. If she married a poor man, or a man dependent on an uncertain income, the sacrifice might be regarded in the light of a sum paid for insurance—the provision of a resource in case of widowhood or other misfortune, which it is well to have in reserve, though it may be still better never to want it.

In the meantime, however, does marriage necessarily involve giving up a profession? On the face of it, judging by existing facts, one would incline to the contrary view. Some of the highest names in literature and art are those of married women; many schoolmistresses are married; clergymen's wives notoriously undertake a large share of extra-domestic work; and there is no evidence that in any of these cases the husbands are neglected, or the children worse brought up than other people's. It seems to be forgotten that women have always been married. Marriage is not a modern discovery, offering a hitherto untrodden field of action for feminine energy. The novelty is, that, as has been said already, the old field has been invaded and taken possession of by machinery. The married ladies of former days, instead of sitting in drawing-rooms, eating the bread of idleness, got through a vast amount of household business, which their successors cannot possibly do, simply because it is not there to be done. An educated woman, of active, methodical habits, blessed with good servants, as good mistresses generally are, finds an hour a day amply sufficient for her housekeeping. Nothing is gained by spreading it out over a longer time.* Allowing a fair margin for what are technically called 'social' claims, there remains a surplus, of course varying very considerably in extent, according to circumstances. The question then arises, whether a married woman, having time and energy to spare, may or may not legitimately spend it, if she likes, either in definitely professional work, or in the unpaid public services, which, when seriously undertaken, constitute something nearly equivalent to a

* On the occasion of a recent vacancy in the secretaryship of a benevolent society several of the candidates were married women. One gave, as her reasons for applying, 'loneliness and want of employment.' In another case, the application was made by a husband on behalf of his wife.

profession. Inasmuch as the adoption of
such a course would most probably effect
some change in the aspect of family life,
it is reasonable to ask whether such change
is likely to be for good or for evil; and
any objections which may suggest themselves ought to be respectfully considered.

One of the most obvious is the fear
that a profession might prove a snare,
leading to the neglect of humbler and
more irksome duties. And it is right to
admit frankly that the apprehension may
not be altogether groundless. M. Simon,
indeed, asserts, with the happy confidence
we are all so apt to display on matters
of which we have had no experience, that
household drudgery, 'though very laborious, is agreeable to women;'[18] and

Sydney Smith has made merry over the notion that a mother would desert an infant for a quadratic equation.[19] And of course, put in that extreme way, the idea is ridiculous. But looking at the case broadly—putting on one side the little fretting cares and worries of domestic life, and on the other the larger and more genial interests of professional work, it may be confessed that a temptation might very possibly arise to shirk the less engaging task. But it does not follow that because a temptation exists, it must be irresistible. To construct a plan of life absolutely free from temptation is a simple impossibility, even supposing it to be desirable. Every career has its snares, and a life of narrow interests and responsibilities is no exception to the rule. The true safeguard seems to consist, not in restraints and limitations, but in a vivid sense of all that is involved in the closer relationships, and in a steadfast habit of submission to duty. In the present case it may be noted that, however fascinating the temptation may be, it is at any rate open and well understood. It is not a pitfall, which any one could walk into unawares through ignorance of its existence. The paramount importance of home duties is enforced by all the sanctions of an overwhelming public opinion. Any neglect is liable to be punished, not only by the immediate discomfort arising from it, but by universal disapproval. An offence against which the warnings are so

trumpet-tongued, and of which the consequences are so thoroughly disagreeable,
can scarcely be very dangerously attrac-
tive.

If it is admitted that professional
women are likely, or at least as likely as
others, to be both able and diligent in the
discharge of family obligations, another
objection may be raised, founded on the
apprehension that a similarity of pursuits
would produce an unpleasant similarity
between men and women.   One of the
most plausible arguments in behalf of dis-
similar education is that which rests on
the general desirableness of variety.   We
do not want to be all alike.   The course
of civilisation tends, it is said, already too
strongly towards uniformity.

' For " ground in yonder social mill,
  We rub each other's angles down,
  And lose," he said, " in form and gloss
  The picturesque of man and man." ' [20]

And if it could be shown that the isolation of the sexes produces variety of the best kind, and to the greatest possible extent, it would no doubt be a strong argument in its favour. But it is questionable whether this is the best means of obtaining variety. As there can be no unanimity on matters of which one party is ignorant, so also, in the same sense, there can be no diversity. We do not obtain two views of a subject by incapacitating one of the parties from taking any view at all. If the differences between men and women are such that they are predisposed to treat whatever comes before them in a somewhat different manner, we shall get greater variety by presenting to both the most important subjects of thought, than by sorting out subjects into classes and submitting each to a kind of class treatment. And so also as to methods of training. It seems likely that a more healthily diversified type of character will be obtained by cultivating the common human element, and leaving individual differences free to develop themselves, than by dividing mankind into two great sections and forcing each into a mould. You may indeed obtain diversity by mutilation or distortion. You may make a girl unlike a boy by shutting her up, giving her insufficient air and exercise, and teaching her that grace and refinement are synonymous with affectation and feebleness. You may make a boy unlike a girl by teaching him to care for nothing but out-of-door sports, and by making him believe that he is showing spirit when he is rude and selfish. But this is not the kind of variety that any one seriously wishes to cultivate.

It may here perhaps be argued on the other hand, that to give wives professions would tend to separate them from their husbands by throwing them into a society of their own, and leading them to set up a distinct set of independent interests,— that whereas a wife now throws herself into her husband's concerns, losing sight of herself in her sympathy with him, she would, if she had a pursuit of her own, be led astray by ambition, occupied with her own aims, absorbed in a current of life apart from his. Here again it may be admitted that the danger might, in very rare cases, possibly exist. But, on the whole, the risk seems to be much more than counterbalanced by a very strong tendency in an exactly opposite direction. In many cases, the profession of both would be the same, judging by present experience. Artists marry artists, clergymen's daughters marry clergymen, literary women often, though not always, marry literary men, medical women would probably marry medical men, and so on. It is likely that a man who chose to marry a professional woman at all would marry in his own profession. But supposing it

were otherwise, a woman who had work
similar, though not in all respects identical
with that of her husband, would be more
able than one whose occupation was of an
entirely alien character, to sympathise
with him in his difficulties and in his suc-
cesses.   She would understand them and
enter into them with a first-hand kind of
interest, fuller and more intelligent, if not
more genuine, than a merely reflected
interest could be.   On the other hand, it
would be at least as easy for a husband to
enter into interests somewhat akin to his
own, as into the small domestic worries
which fill so large a space in the thoughts
and imaginations of women who have
nothing else to occupy them.   There are
many wives who really have very little to

talk to their husbands about, except the virtues or the crimes of servants, and the little gossip of the neighbourhood. If their husbands will not listen to what they have to say on these subjects, they are obliged to take refuge in silence.

The enormous loss to general culture entailed by the solitude of the male intellect is very little thought of. Yet it would seem obvious enough that children brought up in a home where the everyday conversation is of a somewhat thoughtful and literary cast, have an immense start as compared with those who learn nothing unconsciously, and are obliged to gather all their knowledge laboriously from books. Social and domestic intercourse is an educational instrument largely used in

cultivated circles. In the great mass of
English society it is scarcely used at all,
for this obvious reason, that education is
in great part onesided, and the easy inter-
change of thought is therefore impossible.
A slight infusion of an intellectual element
would go far to expel the gossip and the
microscopic criticism of one's neighbours,
which forms so large and so degrading a
part in the domestic talk of the middle
classes. The mental effort need not be a
severe one. Talk may be very small, and
yet have a certain dignity, if it touches
even but lightly on elevating subjects. It
is the effort to draw up conversation from
empty wells that wearies the spirit, and
drives even goodnatured people into
scandal and slander. Contrast the forced

and insipid small talk of ordinary society, resorted to by way of recreation, but in the last degree unrefreshing in its nature, with the spontaneous overflowings of a cultivated mind.

'She spake such good thoughts natural, as if she
    always thought them—
She had sympathies so rapid, open, free as bird on
    branch,
Just as ready to fly east as west, whichever way be-
    sought them,
In the birchen wood a chirrup, or a cock-crow in the
    grange.
In her utmost lightness there is truth—and often she
    speaks lightly,
Has a grace in being gay, which even mournful souls
    approve ;
For the root of some grave earnest thought is under-
    struck so rightly,
As to justify the foliage and the waving flowers above.'[21]

It is in fact as a means of bringing men and women together, and bridging over the intellectual gulf between them, that a more liberal education and a larger scope for women are chiefly to be desired. It has been pointed out by a well-known essayist, that 'the purpose of education is not always to foster natural gifts, but sometimes to bring out faculties that might otherwise remain dormant; and especially so far as to make the persons educated cognisant of excellence in those faculties in others.' And even supposing it could be proved that the separate systems are eminently successful in developing certain peculiarly masculine or feminine gifts, the result would be dearly purchased by the sacrifice of mutual understanding and appreciation.

Oddly enough, it is often assumed that

the only way of getting husbands and
wives to agree is to keep them well apart.
Common ground, it is taken for granted,
must of course be a battle ground.   If the
theory of the peculiarly receptive character
of the female intellect has any truth in it,
it might be expected to be rather the
other way, and that wives would, as a rule,
be only too ready to adopt their husbands'
opinions.   In any case, contact has an
undoubted tendency to produce unanimity, and the chances are therefore in
favour of agreement.   And that there
should be intelligent agreement, a community of thought and feeling, on all
matters of importance, is surely the first
necessity for the healthy and harmonious
development of family life.   M. Simon has

drawn a vivid picture of the influence on
children of discordance between fathers
and mothers, even when there is nothing
like an open rupture.

'Cette femme qu'une religieuse a formée
et cet homme nourri des doctrines de
tolérance, peut-être d'indifférence, mariés
ensemble, sont un vivant anachronisme.
La femme est du dix-septième siècle et
l'homme de la fin du dix-huitième. Admet-
tons qu'ils vivent en bonne intelligence,
elle le croyant damné, lui la jugeant fana-
tique. Qu'arrivera-t-il, quand à leur tour,
ils enseigneront? Et ils enseigneront;
être père, être mère, c'est enseigner. La
mère répétera sa doctrine, puisée au cou-
vent; le père, par prudence, se taira. Se
taira-t-il? Si même il prend cela sur lui,

son silence sera commenté par ses actes.
Et que pensera l'enfant de cette contradiction, aussitôt qu'il pensera ?   Il condam-
nera l'un ou l'autre, peut-être l'un et
l'autre.   Plus il aura l'esprit puissant, plus
vite il perdra respect. . . . Il semble à des
esprits sans portée que l'indifférence et la
foi vivront bien ensemble, parce que l'une
exige et l'autre céde ; mais céder à une
croyance sans l'accepter, c'est ne pas être.
La paix entre deux âmes est possible
quand elle est fondée sur l'identité de foi ;
elle est encore possible quand elle est
fondée sur le respect réciproque d'une foi
diverse et sincère ; mais appeler paix cette
absence de lutte qui naît de l'indifférence,
c'est confondre la paix avec la défaite et la
vie avec le néant.'

The author of 'Vincenzo'[22] has given in
that remarkable story a view too painfully
lifelike to be disbelieved, of the conjugal
misery resulting from a profound disson-
ance between a husband and wife on religious and political questions, and asserts
that the wreck of domestic happiness so
graphically pictured represents a reality
far from uncommon. 'Would to God,'
he exclaims, 'that the case were an isolated one! But no; there is scarcely any
corner in Italy, scarcely any corner in
Europe, that does not exhibit plenty of
such and worse.' Such a state of things
could scarcely exist in England. The
counteracting influences are too many and
too strong. But it cannot be said that we
are exempt from danger. In how many

English families wives and sisters are clinging blindly to traditional beliefs and observances, from which husbands and brothers are turning away with indifference or dislike. How natural the transition from the theory which assigns ' to the one the supremacy of the head, to the other that of the heart '—to that further division which attributes to the one Reason, to the other Faith. Heartless Rationalism and imbecile credulity ! Is it in the union of these feeble and jarring tones that we shall find the full chord of family harmony ? Ought we not rather to turn with suspicion from these artificial attempts to apportion attributes and duties ? May we not welcome, as at least a step in the right direction, a change in our con-

ventional habits, which may extend,
though in ever so small a degree, the region
of common thoughts and aims, common
hopes and disappointments, common joys
and common sorrows ?

CHAPTER VI.

SPECIFIC SUGGESTIONS.

IF it be admitted that the law of human duty is the same for both sexes, and if the specific functions belonging to each demand substantially the same qualities for their performance, it appears to follow that the education required is likely to be, in its broader and more essential features, the same. What that education ought to be has lately been much discussed, but at present without much sign of approaching unanimity. That there should be great difference of opinion is natural, inasmuch as almost every one is inclined to recommend for universal adoption just what he happens to like best himself; while, on the other hand, a few people of a different turn of mind are disposed to undervalue what they possess themselves, and to give extra credit to subjects or methods, the insufficiency of which has not been brought home to them by personal experience. In the education of girls the selection of subjects seems to be directed by no principle whatever. Strong protests are raised against assimilating it to that of boys; but very little is said as to the particulars in which it ought to differ. The present distribution is, indeed, somewhat whimsical. Inasmuch as young men go into offices where they have to conduct foreign correspondence, and, as they travel about all over the world, they are taught the dead languages. As woman's place is the domestic hearth, and as middle class women rarely see a foreigner, they are taught modern languages with a special view to facility in speaking. As men are supposed to work with their heads all day, and have nothing in the world to do when they are indisposed for reading but to smoke or to go to sleep, they are taught neither music nor drawing. As women have always the resource of needlework, they learn music and drawing besides. As women are not expected to take part in political affairs, they are taught history. As men do, boys learn mathematics instead. In physical science, astronomy and botany are considered the ladies' department. Chemistry and mechanics being the branches most directly applicable to domestic uses, are reserved for boys.

These distinctions ought rather, however, to be spoken of as a thing of the past. The educators of boys and girls respectively are learning and borrowing from each other.* An approximation is

* With equal need, if what Lord Russell says is true :—'As it is at present, there is no doubt that women of the higher ranks have much more knowledge and information when their education is finished

already in progress, in which the encroachment, if it be an encroachment,
is chiefly from the side of boys; for
while Latin and mathematics are slowly
making their way into girls' schools, we
find that in the University local examinations, music, drawing, and modern
languages have from the beginning been
recognised as desirable for boys. It is,

than men have. But I cannot see any reason why
our young men should not, while they have the advantage of public schools, at the same time be able to
do a sum in the rule of three, and make themselves
masters of the fact that James I. was not the son of
Queen Elizabeth.'

In another place he says:—'It is to a dogged
application to the Latin grammar perhaps that the
precision of men, when compared to women, in this
country is in great part to be attributed.'—*Earl
Russell on the English Government and Constitution,*
pp. 210, 208. [23]

like most other things, very much a
question of degree. The system of mutual isolation has never been thoroughly
carried out. Even those who hold most
strongly that classics and mathematics
are proper for boys, and modern languages and the fine arts for girls, leave
as common ground the wide field of
English literature, in itself almost an
education. To a large extent men and
women read the same books, magazines,
and newspapers ; and though in the
highest class of literature, written by
scholars for scholars, and, therefore, full
of classical and scientific allusions, there
is much that women only half understand, the deficiency under which they
labour is shared by many male readers.

Probably, after all, it matters less what is nominally taught, than that, whatever it is, it should be taught in the best way. Any subject may be made flat and unprofitable if unintelligently taught ; and, on the other hand, there is scarcely anything which may not be made an instrument of intellectual discipline, if wisely used. Then, again, all branches of knowledge are so closely connected and mutually dependent, that it is scarcely possible to learn anything which will not be found more or less useful hereafter in learning something else. Even the much despised and denounced 'smattering of many things,' has its merits in this way, as well as in giving a certain breadth of vision, by opening vistas into innumerable fields of knowledge, never to be explored by any single human being. The degree in which the study of certain subjects cultivates certain faculties is a matter on which we are far from agreeing. Nor is it decided—in fact we have scarcely begun to discuss—what faculties most need cultivation. In the middle classes the imagination seems to be the one in which the deficiency is most marked. Every now and then some one recommends mathematics for girls as a curb to the imagination. It might be as well first to ascertain whether the imaginations of commonplace girls want to be curbed; whether, on the contrary, they do not want rather to be awakened and set to work, with something to work upon. The business of the imagination is not merely to build castles in the air, though that is, no doubt, a useful and commendable exercise; it has other and most important duties to perform. For, manifestly, an unimaginative person is destitute of one of the main elements of sympathy. Probably, if the truth were known, it would be found that injustice and unkindness are comparatively seldom caused by harshness of disposition. They are the result of an incapacity for imagining ourselves to be somebody else. Any one who has tried it must be aware of the enormous difficulty of conceiving the state of mind of a pauper or a thief. The same difficulty is experienced in a degree by any one in easy circumstances in realising the condition and looking from the point of view of a very poor, or comparatively poor person. It is probably equally difficult to ordinary minds to imagine the condition of always having more money than you quite know what to do with. The absence of sympathy between youth and age is traceable to the same want. Old people have either forgotten their own youth, or they remember it too well, and fall into the not less fatal mistake of supposing that the new youth is like their own. Young people, on their part, are equally at a loss to understand what it is to be old. In all the relations of life, the want of imagination produces defective sympathy, and defective sympathy brings in its train all sorts of vague and intolerable evils. In every branch of study a vivid imagination is a most powerful agent, aiding the memory, and bringing clearly before the mind the materials on which a judgment has to be formed.

This, however, is not the place to discuss the comparative importance of the mental faculties. Without going into the details of what, or how to teach, it will be more to the purpose to inquire whether there are any general measures, the working of which is likely to be beneficial, let the subjects and the methods of instruction be what they may.

Among the most necessary, and the most easily and immediately applicable, is the extension to women of such examinations as demand a high standard of attainment. The test of a searching examination is indispensable as a guarantee for the qualifications of teachers; it is wanted as a stimulus by young women studying with no immediate object in view, and no incentive to exertion other than the high, but dim and distant, purpose of self-culture. This purpose, regarded in its bearing on the general welfare, is indeed honourable and animating, and every other must be subordinate to it. But we must not forget that we have to deal with human and very imperfect beings; and it is not difficult to believe that young women of only average energy and perseverance, while working in the main towards the higher end, may

yet need an occasionally recurring stage
within sight, as an allurement to draw
them on, and to help them in their
struggle with the temptations to indolence
which lie thick about their path.   The
fact of having an examination to work
for, would not only be a stimulus to
themselves, it would also serve as a
defence against idle companions, whose
solicitations it is hard to refuse on the
mere ground of an abstract love of
learning.

The want of examinations for women
is not a new discovery. So long ago as
1841, Dr Arnold wrote to Mr Justice
Coleridge :—' I feel quite as strongly as
you do the extreme difficulty of giving
to girls what really deserves the name of

education intellectually. When —— was young, I used to teach her some Latin with her brothers, and that has been, I think, of real use to her, and she feels it now in reading and translating German, of which she does a great deal. But there is nothing for girls like the Degree examination, which concentrates one's reading so beautifully, and makes one master a certain number of books perfectly. And unless we had a domestic examination for young ladies, to be passed before they come out, and another, like the great go, before they come of age, I do not see how the thing can ever be effected. Seriously, I do not see how we can supply sufficient encouragement for systematic and laborious reading, or how we can insure many things being retained at once fully in the mind, when we are wholly without the machinery which we have for our boys.'

In another letter, speaking of the need of continual questioning in the case of a boy, he says, 'He wants this, and he wants it daily, not only to interest and excite him, but to dispel what is very apt to grow around a lonely reader not constantly questioned—a haze of indistinctness as to a consciousness of his own knowledge or ignorance; he takes a vague impression for a definite one, an imperfect notion for one that is full and complete, and in this way he is continually deceiving himself.'[24]

This is an exact description of the state

of the young female mind, even where there has been considerable cultivation. Women have 'general ideas,' which interest and occupy their minds, but produce little fruit, owing to their incompleteness and uncertainty. Of course, it would be absurd to recommend examinations as an infallible cure for this or any other mental defect. The familiar objections, that there are many things which no examination can test ; that they sometimes encourage cram and check originality ; and that, when abused, they foster ambition, and cause overexcitement and overwork—no doubt have some truth in them. But the question is whether, on the whole, examinations work for good or for evil ; and the testimony of long experience seems to be strongly in their favour. To refuse to test knowledge, because you cannot by the same process judge of moral excellence, is about as wise as to say that a man ought not to eat, because, unless he also takes exercise, he will not be in good health. Cram is no doubt a very bad thing, but it is not a necessary antecedent of examinations; and, after all, there are alternatives worse than cramming. It may be better even to cram than to leave the mind quite empty; and though the word has become, by perpetual reiteration, closely associated with the idea of examinations, it is as well to remember that it is quite possible for knowledge to be equally undigested, whether it has been got up for an examination or not. As to fostering ambition, the

question seems to be, whether it is possible, or even desirable, entirely to eradi-
cate it, and whether to direct it towards
a respectable object, the pursuit of which
at least implies some good moral qualities,
may not be useful as diverting it from
that meanest of aims—the only one held
up indiscriminately to women of every
grade—that of shining in society. The
danger of injury to health, through ex-
citement and overwork, is within the
control of parents and teachers. As regards girls, the experience of the Cambridge local examinations has proved
beyond a doubt that, where ordinary common sense is practised, there is no risk
whatever of this sort.

There are at present no examinations

open to women of such standing as to
constitute a fitting test of advanced
scholarship. The examinations of the
Society of Arts, being primarily intended
for artisans, are manifestly inadequate ;
and the University local examinations
are limited to students under eighteen.
The University of London, having adopted
the principle of making its examinations
simply a test and standard of acquirement, without enforcing upon students
that their knowledge should have been
acquired by attendance at college lectures,
or under any particular system, is in a
peculiarly favourable position for giving
assistance in this matter. The extension
of the London examinations to women
need present no greater difficulties than

those which have been already overcome in throwing open the Cambridge local examinations to girls, and would go far towards supplying a want which every day becomes more pressing.

The access to progressive examinations, of such a character as to test and attest advanced attainments, would, there is every reason to believe, at once begin to work in lengthening the period of study. It would probably tell first upon the ladies' colleges ; but its influence would not be limited to college students. Where circumstances make it inconvenient for a girl to attend classes, it may still be practicable for her to pursue her studies at home, so long as there is some definite and intelligible object in view. An essential requisite is the use of a room where she can be secure from trivial interruptions. This might seem obvious enough ; but those who know anything of family life in the middle class are aware that it is a privilege rarely accorded to young women. The best teaching within reach would, of course, be a great assistance, but would not be in all cases indispensable.

An increase in the number of colleges and a higher standard of efficiency would be the natural result of retaining the students under instruction for a longer time, and this again would improve the quality of teachers. Probably something more would still be required in the way of training for teachers. It seems to be

the opinion of the persons best qualified
to judge, that some technical instruction
is required as a preparation for teaching,
and that such instruction might be obtained by taking a short course at a
training-college at the end of a general
education.[25]

The ladies' colleges may fairly be expected to supply 'the education of a
lady.' The special training for any particular profession must be obtained in
distinct schools. This, of course, applies
to every branch of art. It applies also to
the study of medicine. There is at present no medical school for women ;[26] and
individual students are therefore obliged
to obtain the necessary instruction privately. It is to be wished that one of

the London hospitals, not connected with any existing medical school, should be reserved for female students and classes formed in connexion with it. If this were done, as it probably would be on the application of a sufficient number of students, the education of medical women would be provided for.

The preparation for business is, in most cases, simply a matter of arrangement, requiring nothing but the good will and hearty concurrence of the masters. The easiest thing would be for fathers to bring up their daughters to their own business; and, no doubt, this would often be done, if custom permitted. It is the fear of public opinion—of exciting astonishment and remark—that, probably more than any other cause, imposes upon parents what they feel to be a sort of moral and social obligation to keep their daughters idle.

In addition to other hindrances in the way of giving a thorough education to girls, there is one which presses heavily on persons of narrow incomes—namely, its costliness as compared with that of boys. This is a fact, notwithstanding the other fact, that the teachers of girls are, as a rule, much worse paid than the teachers of boys. It is traceable to two causes—the absence of endowments, and the smallness of girls' schools. Both these causes are removable.

With regard to endowments, there is reason to believe that a large proportion of those which are now appropriated to the use of boys were originally intended for both sexes. The founders do not seem to have known anything about the modern theories of separate education, and, when they established a school, had no idea of excluding any of ' the children' of the parish or kin which it was designed to benefit. It is noticeable that, in cases where girls happen to be expressly mentioned in the foundation deeds, Latin and accounts are almost invariably named in the course of instruction laid down. There is much difference of opinion as to the permanent usefulness of endowments. Some people think they do more harm than good, and would like to get rid of them altogether. This seems a somewhat extreme view; and, at any rate, as the endowments exist, something must be done with them. If it is for the general good that education should be much more expensive, and, therefore, much more difficult to get, for a girl than for a boy; or if the balance is redressed by greater willingness on the part of parents to make sacrifices in behalf of their daughters, it may be well to let the present distribution stand. But it appears rather that the education of women is at present exactly at the stage at which artificial support is wanted. There are many ways in which it might be applied. Probably the most useful at the present juncture would be the foundation of exhibitions and scholarships, awarded under such varying conditions as to give them the widest possible range. Taking the middle classes generally, there seems to be no reason why they should not pay for the education of their children at cost price ; but there are many exceptions, and the legitimate use of all eleemosynary aid seems to be to meet special cases of misfortune.   For this reason it is desirable that, besides exhibitions and scholarships awarded after a competitive examination —which would act as an encouragement to industry and ability—there should be in the hands of governors and trustees a power of conferring free or assisted education without competition.   Scholarships might be tenable at elementary schools, at a college, at a medical school, or at schools of art ; or there might be exhibitions available for apprenticeship to any profession or trade whatsoever, at the discretion of the trustees.

In the meantime, without any aid from public sources, a good deal might be done by a more judicious use of existing means. The present mode of carrying on girls' schools involves an enormous waste of teaching power. Fifteen or twenty girls absorb a staff amply sufficient for three or four times the number. This is inevitable in small schools; and the consequence follows, that in many boarding-schools for girls the terms are considerably higher than at Rugby or Harrow. It is doubtful whether very large boarding-schools would work well; but the difficulty may be got over in another way, by establishing a thoroughly good day-school, and clustering round it boarding-houses of moderate size, according to the demand. In places like Blackheath, Clapham, St John's Wood, or in any locality where girls' schools congregate, this plan might be adopted, and would combine many of the respective advantages of large and small schools. The facilities for classification, companionship in study, healthy public spirit, and a general kind of open-airiness which go with large numbers, would be found in the school. The boardinghouses would have the quietness and something of the domestic character which it is difficult to get in a household conducted on a very large scale. The popularity of small boarding-schools is probably chiefly owing to their fancied resemblance to a home circle. There is an impression that a group of girls, all about the same age, and without father or brothers, constitute something like a family. It is really much more like a nunnery ; and there is reason to believe that, in a less degree, just those evils which are said to attach to conventual life are rife in boardingschools.

A sense of these evils leads some people to prefer the system of private governesses. This no doubt has recommendation ; it certainly has serious drawbacks. Among those which are inevitable is the effect of a lonely life on the governess. Without going into sentimental wailings over her unhappy lot, it must be confessed that her position is peculiarly isolated

She spends the greater part of her time in intercourse with young and immature minds, only varied by unequal association with the parents or grown-up brothers and sisters of her pupils. The society of her equals in age and position is entirely wanting, and the natural tendency of such mental solitude is to produce childishness, angularity, and narrow-mindedness. It must be a very strong character indeed which can do without the wholesome trituration and the expansive influence of equal companionship, and this is just what a governess cannot have. A great effort may be made to treat her as one of the family, but she does not really belong to the people, or even to their class. She is always a bird of passage, and in this respect her position is worse than that of a servant, who, besides having the companionship of fellowservants, may look forward to remaining in one family for life. A governess must always be prepared to leave when the term of temporary service expires, and this is in itself an obstacle to the formation of strong attachments. And if it is true that the conditions of governess life have a deteriorating effect on character, it follows that the pupils will in a degree more or less be losers. Whether there may be advantages or conveniences which more than compensate for what is lost, is a question which must be affected by considerations varying in individual cases. Similarly, with regard to boardingschools, a first-rate mistress may be able to offer certain advantages attainable in no other way. The conclusion arrived at goes no farther than this, that, other things being equal, a large day-school attended by scholars living either at home or in small boardinghouses, has a clear advantage, both as regards economy and mental and moral training, over the rival systems of boardingschools and private governesses. It follows that in any direct efforts which may be made for the improvement of elementary education, the foundation or strengthening of well conducted dayschools is the wisest course to adopt.

The foregoing suggestions must of course be subject to all sorts of modifications, according to temporary and local necessities. Specific schemes, adapted to circumstances, will be devised as occasions arise. In the meantime, any kind of recognition of the fact that the education of women is a matter worth thinking about, is of the utmost practical value. In this point of view, as indicating and expressing a growing sense of the importance of the subject, the extension to girls of the local examinations of the Universities of Cambridge and Edinburgh, and the steps taken by the Schools Inquiry Commission in their pending investigations, have an indirect influence quite out of proportion to the immediate and calculable results obtained, affording a moral support and encouragement the effect of which it is not easy to estimate.

CHAPTER VII.

CONCLUSION.

TO guard against misconception on so obscure and so complex a subject as that of the present inquiry is a somewhat hopeless endeavour. But it may, perhaps, be worth while to say once more, what has so often been said already, that those who ask for a fuller and freer life for women have no desire to interfere with distinctions of sex.

The question under debate is not whether, as a matter of fact, there is such a thing as distinctive manhood and womanhood; for that no one denies. The dispute is rather as to the degree in which certain qualities, commonly regarded as respectively masculine and feminine characteristics, are such intrinsically, or only conventionally; and further, as to the degree of prominence which it is desirable to give to the specific differences in determining social arrangements. It is not against the recognition of real distinctions, but against arbitrary judgments, not based upon reason, that the protest is raised. If, in the exigencies of controversy, expressions may sometimes be used which seem to involve a denial of differ-

ences in the respective natures of women
and of men, it must be regarded as a misfortune for which the advocates of re-
striction and suppression are responsible.
When broad assertions are made as to
natural fitness and unfitness, and a course
of action is founded upon them, it becomes necessary, at least, to ask for proof.
When proof is wanting, it is not un-
natural to fall back upon feeling; and
prejudices, dignified by the name of instincts, are appealed to as decisive when
rational argument fails. The whole question is clouded over by this confusing
procedure. The instincts, to which so
much importance is attached, differ in the
most bewildering manner. What one
person's instinct pronounces lawful and

becoming, another finds revolting. As-
sumptions are made, and a fabric of
argument is built up upon data which
are unverified, and which it is at present
impossible either to verify or absolutely
to contradict. For, until artificial appli-
ances are removed, we cannot know
anything certainly about the native distinctions. As to the future, who can
say? It may be that,

'In the long years liker must they grow,
 The man be more of woman, she of man;
 He gain in sweetness and in moral height,
 Nor lose the wrestling thews that throw the world;
 She mental breadth, nor fail in childward care;
 More as the double-natured poet each :' [27]

or it may be that, when 'full-summed in
all their powers,' new shades of unlike-
ness—refinements of diversity hitherto

unimagined—may appear. It is neither
necessary nor expedient to prejudge the
question ; and those whose faith in the
reality and permanence of the native distinctions is the strongest are the least
tempted to make rash assertions on either
side.   The excessive apprehensiveness
shown by some people on this point
seems to indicate a deeprooted distrust
in the strength of their position.   The
fear betrays a doubt. No one urges that
girls should be denied the use of cold
water, or fresh air, or light, or animal
food, lest they should grow into boys.
Yet that these conditions tend to produce masculine vigour cannot be denied.
Those who are afraid that a free range
of thought and action would injure the

delicacy of the female mind, ought, in consistency, to carry their precautions a little farther. The atmosphere of a hothouse, judiciously darkened, abstinence from exercise, and a vegetarian diet would have an evident tendency to produce a sickly delicacy of complexion, to give languor to the limbs, and feebleness to the voice, and in every way to make girls much more unlike their brothers than they were by nature. And if this is the object of education, the appropriate means ought to be used.

In the meantime, a great part of the difficulties which beset every question concerning women would be at once removed by a frank recognition of the fact, that there is between the sexes a deep and broad basis of likeness. The hypothesis that men and women are essentially and radically different, embarrasses every discussion. When facts are proved and admitted, scarcely any progress has been made, because it is assumed that their action is modified by their application to the feminine nature. Conditions which would certainly make a man happy or miserable, as the case might be, are supposed to have a different, if not an exactly opposite, effect upon a woman. The theory has been asserted and reasserted so incessantly, that even women themselves have been partly persuaded to believe it. And it is, no doubt, so far true, that while the education and the circumstances of women are widely differ-

ent from those of men, every agency
brought to bear upon either must act
somewhat differently. But to create facts,
and then to argue from them as if they
were the result of an unalterable destiny,
is a method which convinces only so long
as it is enforced by prejudice. 'Chacun
selon sa capacité'—'à chaque produc-
teur l'ouvrage auquel il est propre'—these
are maxims of unquestioned validity. But
who shall say for another—much more,
who shall say for half the human race
—this, or this, is the measure of your
capacity; this, and no other, is the work
you are qualified to perform? 'Women's
work,' it is said, 'is helping work.' Certainly it is. And is it men's work to
hinder? The vague information that wo-

men are to be ministering angels is no
answer to the practical questions, Whom
are they to help, and how ?   The easy
solution, that it is their nature to do
what men cannot do, or cannot do so
well, has never been adopted in practice,
inasmuch as everything in the world that
there is to do, the care of infants alone
excepted, men are doing ; and there is
nothing that a trained man cannot do
better than an untrained woman.   Literature and art, teaching, nursing, cooking,
sewing—these are the recognised feminine
occupations, and they are all shared by
men.   The pursuit of them does not turn
men into women, or women into men.
Miss Yonge and Mrs Oliphant[28]' help '
Mr Trollope in supplying the world with

novels; and it is not thought necessary to guard either party from writing masculine or feminine novels respectively. Schoolmasters and schoolmistresses do not come into unseemly rivalry, although women teach boys and men teach girls. By and by it will be found equally superfluous to prescribe limitations in any department of thought or industry.

It can scarcely be necessary to discuss at length the difficulty expressed in the frequent question,—if women take to doing men's work, what are men to do? Will not the intrusion of women into professions and trades already overcrowded, lower the current rate of wages, and by thus making men less able to support their families—in the long run, do more

harm than good ?   As to the manner and
degree in which the labour-market might
be affected by such a readjustment as is
proposed, it is difficult to predict anything with certainty.   It is impossible to
tell beforehand how many women would
take to what is called (by a very con-
spicuous *petitio principii*) men's work,
and how large a portion of their lives
they would devote to it.   If women,
already destined to work for their bread,
chose to earn it in some hitherto unac-
customed way, it is obvious that in the
exact measure in which their entrance
into a new profession reduced the rate
of wages in that particular calling, it
would tend to raise it in some other
which they would have otherwise pur-

sued, and the balance would thus be redressed. If, on the other hand, women are not supporting themselves, they are being supported · by somebody else, consuming either present earnings or accumulated savings. To keep them from earning money does not prevent their spending it. Let us suppose the event, not a very probable one, that the introduction of women into the medical profession would lower the average rate of remuneration by one-third, in which case the professional income of an ordinary medical man would be lessened in the same proportion. Let us suppose, also —a not at all improbable case—that the doctor's wife, or sister, or daughter, would earn, in the practice of *her* pro-

fession, a sum equivalent to the one-
third he has lost. Evidently, the doctor
and his family would be where they
were, neither better nor worse off than
before. In the meantime, the public
would be so much the richer by getting
its medical attendance one-third cheaper.
Whatever might be the temporary effect
of opening any particular profession to
women, one thing is certain, it can never
be for the interest of society, in a purely
economical aspect, to keep any class of
its members in idleness. A man who
should carry one of his arms in a sling,
in order to secure greater efficiency and
importance to the other, would be regarded as a lunatic. The one free member might very probably gain a little

extra dexterity, of an abnormal sort, but that the man would be on the whole a loser, is obvious. The case of the body politic is precisely analogous. The economical argument is all in favour of setting everybody to work. Such difficulties as exist are of a moral or æsthetic nature, and require for their disentanglement considerations of a different sort from those which govern the comparatively easy economical question.

Much misapprehension has probably arisen from a confusion between a standard or law of life and the persons to whom it is applied. A standard or law says nothing about the character of the persons who are expected to conform to it. It pronounces no opinion upon

their nature beyond what is implied in
assuming it to be not impossible for them
to live by it. The command, 'Thou
shalt love the Lord thy God with all
thy heart, and thy neighbour as thy-
self,' implies that such love is possible to
men ; but it may be manifested in count-
less ways—in heroic conflict or in patient
endurance, in passionate ardour or meek
submission. If it be true that certain
gifts and graces are specially congenial
to the masculine or feminine nature, the
presentation of a common standard will
draw them out according to their kind,
without the risk of seeming to dispense
with the less easy virtues. Just as when
you plant two rose-trees in the same
ground, you imply the belief that certain

general conditions of soil and atmosphere
are good for both, but you make no
attempt to influence variations of colour
or of perfume; so the Christian theory
of education implies an essential resemblance between the sexes, without inter-
fering in any way with native differences.
If, indeed, you adopt the analogy, not
without a certain fanciful charm, according to which men are trees and women
flowers,[29] the separate system is right.
You do wisely to plant the oak in the
forest, and to shelter the delicate gera-
nium in the hothouse. But this view
implies that men and women are of a
different genus, which no one in his
senses would maintain. The popular
simile of the oak and the ivy is equally

untenable. Advocates on both sides are apt to talk as if men and women were distinct races, handing down their respective characteristics from generation to generation. The fact is, as every one knows, that hereditary qualities are transmitted from father to daughter, and from mother to son, with much impartiality. The influences tending to create dissimilarity, which, in our day at least, are at work, without a moment's intermission, from the cradle to the grave, are incessantly neutralised in each successive generation. If it were not so, it is difficult to imagine what the human race would become. One thing is certain, it would very soon cease to be human.

Writers on this subject commonly adopt

somewhat of a threatening tone in reference to any proposed change. They warn women that if the oak and ivy theory is given up, what is called the old chivalry will die out, and they must no longer expect to be protected. And it is further urged that men would suffer, no less than women, from the absence of any demand upon their protective instincts. We are indebted to Mr Kingsley for a very clear and moderate statement of this view in a chapter of 'The Roman and the Teuton' on the Lombard Laws.

'It is to be remarked,' he says, 'that no free woman can live in Lombardy, or, I believe, in any Teutonic state, save under the "mundium" of some one. You should understand this word "mund."

Among most of the Teutonic races, women, slaves and youths, at least not of age to carry arms, were under the mund of some one. Of course, primarily the father, head of the family, and if he died, an uncle, elder brother, &c. The married woman was, of course, under the mund of her husband. He was answerable for the good conduct of all under his mund; he had to pay their fines if they offended; and he was bound, on the other hand, to protect them by all lawful means.

'This system still lingers in the legal status of women in England, for good and evil; the husband is more or less answerable for the wife's debts; the wife, till lately, was unable to gain property apart from her husband's control; the wife is supposed, in certain cases of law, to act under the husband's compulsion. All these, and many others, are relics of the old system of mund for women; and that system has, I verily believe, succeeded. It has called out, as no other system could have done, chivalry in the man. It has made him feel it a duty and an honour to protect the physically weaker sex. It has made the woman feel that her influence, whether in the state or in the family, is to be not physical and legal, but moral and spiritual; and that it therefore rests on a ground really nobler and deeper than that of the man. The modern experiments for emancipating women from all mund, and placing them on a physical and legal equality with the man, may be right, and may be ultimately successful. We must not hastily prejudge them. But of this we may be almost certain, that, if they succeed, they will cause a widespread revolution in society, of which the patent danger will be, the destruction of the feeling of chivalry, and the consequent brutalisation of the male sex.'[30]

These are terrible warnings, and may well make any one hesitate in lifting a finger to aid in a revolution charged with such disastrous possibilities. But is it really true that the male sex is likely to be brutalised by learning that a man must no longer rely upon physical and legal influence, but must rest his claims to allegiance on a moral and spiritual basis? Is it good for a man to feel that his influence rests

on a ground less noble and deep than that
of women, and to satisfy himself with a
lower moral position ?   The mund system
may have succeeded,—in other words, it
may have been the best thing possible, in
a rude and barbarous age, when serfdom
also was in full force and 'succeeded' in
its way—a time when force was met by
force, and individual protection was a
surer resource than that of law.   But
even as applying to those days, the success of the system seems to have been
somewhat incomplete.   How it worked—
or failed to work—Mr Kingsley shows in
a few graphic lines, in his recent tale,
'Hereward.'   Describing the fate of the
little Torfrida, his hero's daughter, he
tells us, that 'she was married to Hugh

of Evermue, who is not said to have kicked her; and was, according to them of Crowland, a good friend to their monastery, and therefore, doubtless, a good man. Once, says wicked report, he offered to strike her, as was the fashion in those chivalrous days. Whereon she turned upon him like a tigress, and bidding him remember that she was the daughter of Hereward and Torfrida, gave him such a beating, that he, not wishing to draw sword upon her, surrendered at discretion; and they lived all their lives afterwards as happily as most other people in those times.'[31]

Mr Gladstone lays down, that 'as the law of force is the law of the brute creation, so in proportion as he is under the yoke of that law does man approximate to the brute; and in proportion, on the other hand, as he has escaped from its dominion, is he ascending into the higher sphere of being and claiming relationship with Deity. But the emancipation and due ascendancy of women are not a mere fact : they are the emphatic assertion of a principle; and that principle is the dethronement of the law of force, and the enthronement of other and higher laws in its place, and in its despite.[32] The advocates of the protective theory seem scarcely to have realised that the idea of protection implies the corresponding idea of attack. It assumes, as part of its essence, that somebody is attacking, or what occasion would there be for defence ?

Might it not be well for everybody to abandon the attitude of attack? To assert that in a civilised country women want such protection as any human arm can give, is a contradiction in terms. It is supposing, either that the law permits outrages upon the defenceless, or that it can be broken with impunity. That we in England are as yet only partially emerged from barbarism is indeed true. The time-honoured customs handed down from the days of Hugh of Evermue have not yet disappeared, and cases of assault, almost invariably committed by the natural protector, are not uncommon in English households. But the law undertakes to interfere — and does interfere, though as yet in a somewhat impotent

manner—for the defence of hapless wives
and children. It can scarcely be the true
policy of an age which professes to be
enlightened and humane, to suffer general
licence to prevail, in order that a few rare
souls, able to be a law to themselves and
other people, may have the occasion for
displaying exceptional heroism. If the
scheme of Divine Providence requires
that there should be outlets for the protective energies, they are likely to be
found for a long time yet, in the infir-
mities of age, of infancy, and of poverty,
without encouraging morbid or affected
weakness in human beings intended by
nature to be healthy and strong. There
is still plenty of fighting to do, though
the progress of civilisation has removed

the warfare into new fields, and demands new weapons. Evil now appears in a subtle, intangible shape, against which physical strength is of little avail. But the generosity and the courage which constituted the true beauty and worth of chivalry can never become obsolete. The chivalrous spirit now shows itself in the abandonment of unjust privileges, in the enactment of equal laws, and in facing ridicule, opposition, and discouragement in behalf of unpopular ideas. The great battle between good and evil is for ever going on. The form is renewed from age to age, but the spirit is the same. Let us take care lest, in clinging to forms from which the spirit has departed, in shutting our eyes to keep out the dawning day, we may be blindly fighting the battle of the Philistines,[33] all unwittingly ranged among the enemies of the cause we desire to serve.

1. The educational work of F.D. Maurice (1805-72) was influenced by the hope of counteracting the secularist tendencies of Owenism and Chartism: in 1854 he founded the Working Men's College in Great Ormond Street, a pioneering venture in adult education. Miss Davies presumably did not mean to question his personal commitment to women's education, which had arisen through the work of his sister Mary who kept a school in Southampton. Maurice stated in a course of lectures delivered in 1855, 'If I did not believe that the education of working men would lead us by the most direct route to the education of working women, I should care much less for it'; W.E. Styler (ed.), *Learning and Working* (1968), p.62.

2. ed. J.A. St. John, *The Prose Works of John Milton*, vol.III (London, 1848), 'On Education', pp.464, 467.

3. See, for example, Tennyson, *The Princess* (1847) and Ruskin, 'Of Queen's Gardens', in *Sesame and Lilies* (1865). Despite their sentimental treatment of gender roles and women's education, both Tennyson and Ruskin signed the 'Memorial respecting Need of Place of Higher Education for Girls' got up by Miss Davies and the London Schoolmistresses' Association and presented to the Schools' Inquiry Commission in 1867. *The*

Princess had given the notion of women's colleges, 'With prudes for proctors, dowagers for deans, And sweet girl graduates in their golden hair', connotations of romantic absurdity. For the view that Tennyson, who had come under Maurice's influence in the Cambridge Apostles Society, nevertheless saw the poem as 'a serious attempt, artfully disguised, to change an outworn attitude to an important human problem', see J. Kilham, *Tennyson and the Princess. Reflection of an Age* (1958).

4. Trollope had met Emily Davies through Emily Faithfull, 'that female Caxton of the Age', but his views on women remained unchanged. See 'The Rights of Women' in *North America* (1862) and his lecture on 'The Higher Education of Women' (n.d. 1868-70), which may have been intended as a reply to her book; N. John Hall (ed.), *The Letters of Anthony Trollope.* (Stanford, 1983), 2 vols. pp.220, 996.

5. Sir Arthur Helps (1813-75), clerk of the privy council and man of letters, whose series of dialogues on social and intellectual topics, *Friends in Council* (1847-59), reached a wide public.

6. A public fund of £45,000, collected as a thank-offering to Florence Nightingale for her work in the Crimea, was used to found a training school for nurses at St. Thomas's Hospital in 1860. Various factors combined, however, to create a distance between the

Langham Place circle and Miss Nightingale. Although
she was a cousin of the Leigh Smith sisters, their
illegitimacy had prevented the two families from
associating. Nor did Emily Davies take an interest in
nursing education. 'The business of a hired nurse cannot
be looked upon as a profession for a lady.... The
position of a nurse is in every way too nearly allied to
that of an upper servant to be in the least appropriate
for the daughters and sisters of the mercantile and
professional classes'; Medicine as a Profession for
Women', in *Thoughts on Some Questions Relating to
Women.*

7. Coventry Patmore, *The Victories of Love* (1862),
Book II, viii.

8. Tennyson, 'Isabel' (1830). In this poem 'the poet's
mother was more or less described'; C. Ricks (ed.), *The
Poems of Tennyson* (1969), p.183.

9. Shakespeare, *Henry VIII*, Act II, scene iv.

10. *The Works of George Herbert in Prose and Verse*
(1846), vol.i, p.171.

11. *Sydonie's Dowry*, by the author of *Mademoiselle
Mori* [Miss Roberts], (London, 1865).

12. Lucy Aikin, 1781-1864, historical writer and biogra-
pher, daughter of the Unitarian physician and writer,
John Aikin. She began her literary career at the age of
17 and was proficient in French, Italian and Latin; P.H.

Le Breton, *Memoirs, Miscellanies and Letters of the late Lucy Aikin* (1864).

13. Frederick William Robertson, 1816-53, clergyman, whose reputation as preacher at Trinity chapel, Brighton led to the posthumous publication of sermons and lectures which went through many editions.

14. See above, p.2.

15. Elizabeth Garrett was awarded a license by the Society of Apothecaries in 1865 and became the second woman to have her name on the British Medical Register (the first, Elizabeth Blackwell, had qualified as a graduate of Geneva university). In 1868, however, the Apothecaries restricted entry to their examinations to candidates from the medical schools, then closed to women, and the legal power of other medical examining bodies to examine women remained in doubt until an Enabling Act was passed in 1876. Sophia Jex Blake became in 1877 the first woman to qualify under this Act.

16. The Poor Law Board resisted pressure in the 1860s from Louisa Twining, secretary of the Workhouse Visiting Society, to admit women to salaried posts as workhouse inspectors. The principle was not conceded until 1874, when Mrs Nassau Senior was appointed inspector of workhouse schools.

17. The S.P.E.W. held classes to prepare girls for

commercial careers. Clerical and shop work, largely confined to men in the 1860s, became the fastest growing categories of women's work in the next half century. See L. Holcomb, *Victorian Ladies at Work. Middle Class Working Women in England and Wales, 1850-1914* (1973).

18. Jules Simon, 1814-96, philosopher and politician, minister of public instruction in the early years of the French Third Republic and a firm believer in restricting women to the home.

19. *The Works of the Rev. Sydney Smith* (1859), vol.1, p.177, 'Female Education'. Sydney Smith (1771-1845), a trenchant critic of evangelicalism, ended his life as canon of St. Paul's. He made his name by 'vigorously defending doctrines then unpopular, and now generally accepted' (Leslie Stephen's assessment, *D.N.B.* vol. xviii) in the *Edinburgh Review*, which published this essay in 1809.

20. Tennyson, *In Memoriam* (1850), lxxxix.

21. Elizabeth Barrett Browning, *Lady Geraldine's Courtship* (1844), stanzas 46-7.

22. *Vincenzo, or Sunken Rocks*, by John Ruffini (1807-1881), 3 vols, London 1863.

23. Earl Russell's eldest son, John, Viscount Amberley, married Kate Stanley (1842-74), an active figure in the women's movement in the 1860s and, together with her

mother Lady Stanley of Alderley, a benefactor of Girton College.

24. A.P. Stanley, *The Life of Thomas Arnold DD* (1903 edn), pp.280, 102.

25. In her evidence to the Schools' Inquiry Commission, Miss Davies had opposed the suggestion that middle-class schoolmistresses should be educated in vocationally oriented teacher-training colleges like those that produced elementary schoolteachers; Beale (ed.), *Reports*, p.185.

26. The first was the London Medical School for Women, founded by Sophia Jex Blake in 1874 and, from 1877, associated for clinical training with the London (later Royal) Free Hospital.

27. Tennyson, *The Princess*, vii.

28. Both of whom shared Trollope's distaste for the aspirations of the women's movement; see C.M. Yonge, *The Clever Woman of the Family* (1865), M.O. Oliphant, *Miss Marjoribanks* (1866).

29. Suggested by Professor J.S. Blackie of Edinburgh University: M. St. John Packe, *The Life of John Stuart Mill* (London, 1954), p.496.

30. C. Kingsley, *The Roman and the Teuton. A Series of Lectures Delivered before the University of Cambridge* (1864), pp.281-3.

31. C. Kingsley, *Hereward the Wake* (1866), vol.ii, p.345. Kingsley's ambivalence towards the women's movement appears in *Charles Kingsley. His Letters and Memories of His Life* edited by his wife (1883), pp.294, 302-6.

32. These remarks are taken from Gladstone's address as Lord Rector of Edinburgh University in 1865, 'The place of ancient Greece in the providential order of the world', reprinted in *Gleanings of Past Years* (1879), vol.vii, p.65. Though never a supporter of women's suffrage, Gladstone favoured women's employment and education; his daughter, Helen, became a student and in 1882 vice-principal at Newnham College, Cambridge.

33. A favourite metaphor of Matthew Arnold's. Arnold was among those to whom Miss Davies sent the book; 'very pleasantly written as well as full of things that are true' was his comment. Two years earlier he had been less than encouraging towards her efforts to get girls' schools included in the work of the Schools' Inquiry Commission; Stephen, *Emily Davies*, pp.130-1, 145.